Table of Contents

CONCLUSION

INTRODUCTION

A narcissist has two selves: a true-self and a false-self. The forming of a false self is actually the creation of the Narcissist. The false-self is created and developed and, in turn, it stops the true-self from growing. The true self becomes paralyzed and it plays no role in the life of a narcissist. The true-self of a narcissist is weak, which is why it does not battle the false-self for dominance. The false-self protects the true-self from the emotional pain that would destroy it. The false-self is created because of emotional trauma or a life crisis that the narcissist had to go through. The trauma was so much that the true-self could not handle it, so the false-self was created to protect the true-self from the harm.

The false-self has two major roles to play in the narcissist's life:

1. The false-self is, to the narcissist, their true-self. To the narcissist, the false-self is who they truly are and their true-self

isn't real. The false-self is set up to be a better, unique version of what the narcissist wants to be and, because of this, they believe that their false-self is owed and deserves better treatment.

2. The false-self acts as a shield or proxy for the true-self. It is there to absorb any negative energy, pain, or hardship that the narcissist is exposed to. The true-self is vulnerable and fragile. The reason the false-self was created by the narcissist is likely due to some form of abuse. Therefore, it is there to protect the true-self from that same abuse that would break it further.

These two major roles are important to the narcissist's very existence. If the false-self isn't able to function in this way, then the survival of the true-self is impossible. However, in the narcissist's eye, their true-self is the lesser of the two. The false-self is the most important part of them and they pay no attention to their broken true-self.

There are many different degrees of narcissistic personality disorder, and the false-self exists in all of them. The severity of the false-self versus the true-self is dependent on the severity of the NPD.

In some narcissists, the true-self can overtake the false-self to some degree. This is a sign that the narcissist has a chance to become a normal person and defeat their illness. Some people have witnessed the narcissist's true-self, and this is possible.

The different degrees and severities of narcissistic personality disorder means that some people may appear to be suffering from full-fledged narcissism, but their condition is not as extreme as it seems. With these people, the true-self is still existent. It is possible to observe this true-self, and it may even serve as hope that they can overcome or deal with their condition.

On the other hand, full-fledged narcissism does exist, and the people who suffer from it are a very different story. Narcissists are known to get into depressive moods and have suicidal thoughts. However, there aren't actually very many attempted or successful suicides when it comes to narcissists.

This is because their true-self is already dead. In full-fledged narcissists, the true-self no longer exists inside them and is just an empty husk hiding behind the false-self. Narcissists are the real-life zombies.

With full-fledged narcissism where the true-self is non-existent, the false-self takes the form of the true-self by imitating it. This happens in two steps: the false-self re-interprets emotions and reactions it learns from others, and then it emulates them.

The narcissist re-interprets emotions in a way that is more acceptable for them. They will misinterpret guilt as compassion, or fear as humiliation. This makes it easier for the narcissist's false-self to function in social situations and around other people. Re-interpreting the emotions and reactions this way makes it possible for the narcissist to feed their fantasy world.

Because the narcissist's true-self is no longer existent, the false-self needs to step in and emulate the emotions that its true-self would usually feel. The narcissist has an extraordinary ability to fake empathy and emotions.

The false-self remembers the way people act depending on their state of mind or the situation they're in, and it constructs a way to copy them. It normally results in an unbelievably accurate rendition of a healthy, normally-functioning person's emotional behavior.

It is as if they have all the normal emotions and reactions to certain situations and events stored in drawers, and when they need one, they just open the drawer and grab one. This is how a full-fledged narcissist functions day to day with their false-self deceiving everyone around them.

Most of the time, when narcissistic personality disorder gets this far, a therapist won't bother trying to save the narcissist's true-self. Their true-self is too far gone. Instead, a therapist will focus on building up a new true-self for the narcissist and, hopefully, this new self will be healthy enough and strong enough to fight back against the false-self until it is non-existent.

CHAPTER 1

WHAT IS NARCISSIST ABUSE

Narcissistic abuse is any kind of abuse that is inflicted on a person by a narcissistic person. Unfortunately, many victims of narcissistic abuse are never aware that they have been abused. The only evidence that shows up in their life is the signs of the abuse. If a victim of narcissistic abuse does not realize the extent of the damage, they may eventually give up on life to the extent of committing suicide.

Narcissistic abuses vary in extent. Some narcissists are not violent but only use verbal abuses. Things get worse if a narcissist uses both verbal and violent waves of abuse. Narcissistic abuses target the mind, emotions, and the body. They will inflict physical, mental and emotional pain. The effects of any type of narcissistic abuse are far-reaching. The victims eventually suffer from Narcissistic Abuse Syndrome, PTSD, Anxiety or some mental disorder in their life. It becomes difficult for a person to have a normal life after experiencing narcissistic abuse. However, the extent of the damage also depends on the period under which the person was a captive.

Narcissistic abuse effects are usually far-reaching because torture is applied over time. Some individuals are held hostage by narcissists for decades. Being in the presence of a narcissist for such a long time eventually changes a person's perception of life to the fullest. Victims lose faith in humanity and lack trust in everyone. Even people who believed in love and trust, eventually lose their faith in such. Some victims go the extent of losing faith in God. If the torture goes on for a long time, victims usually result in suicide.

Understanding narcissistic abuses should help anyone in a narcissist relationship or family spot the red flags. Some of the narcissistic abuses may sound so innocent. However, when the abuses are inflicted on an individual over a long time, they take root. Narcissists target a person's values and beliefs. They inflict pain that eventually makes the victims feel worthless and lose their beliefs. If a person undergoes verbal abuse that gives them such an identity, he/she might end up believing the lies perpetuated by the abuser. Victims of narcissistic abuse lose self-esteem and self-worth.

Once the abusive words get into a person's mind, the victim no longer sees a reason to live. They do not live because they want to but only to please the narcissist. They give up on fighting for their dreams or anything they desire. A person who has undergone narcissistic abuse eventually agrees that the narcissist is better and superior.

Spotting narcissistic abuses should not be difficult if you have an idea of what narcissist does. They are all geared towards glorifying the narcissist while demeaning the victim. A narcissist uses words of abuse that directly kill a person's self-worth. They directly inflict pain using suggestions, actions, and words that humiliate and publicly shame the victims. Narcissists try to look good in the eye of the public and use their victims to do whatever they want. They work hard to hide their true identity by forcing, manipulating, and torturing their victims to do certain things.

One clear sign of narcissistic abuse is that the abuser does not have empathy. They may appear to show remorse later on but they surely enjoy inflicting pain. In most cases, they show satisfaction and fulfillment while inflicting the pain. They laugh, smile, and enjoy the suffering in of the victims all ways. When the victim is in pain and begging for mercy, the narcissist swims at the moment and glorifies his/ her personality. They do not show mercy or any feelings of empathy towards their victims. The first step to spotting narcissistic abuse is to identify the sociopathic characteristic of the abuse. Just like sociopaths, narcissists are dead on the inside.

They do not mind hurting or inflicting pain. The only difference between sociopaths and narcissists it's that sociopaths are not attached to the victim. Sociopaths can easily dump the victim and pic another to fulfill their desires. On the other hand, narcissists are attached to the victim for a long time, even for life. Narcissists will break up with someone for years and go back looking for the same person.

When a narcissist believes that someone is their gateway to something they want, they will keep on going back to their victim. They do not give up until they get that person to be a total slave. They use different types of manipulation, including seduction to get the person they want in the place they want.

Types of Narcissistic Abuse

Verbal Abuse

Verbal abuse is the most common type of abuse among narcissists. Before they get to violence, narcissists start being abusive to an individual verbally. They use words that affect the victim's emotions and mental capacity. The characteristics of narcissistic verbal abuses include belittling, accusations, shaming, blaming, bullying, threatening, ordering, sarcasm, criticizing, undermining, opposing, blocking, interrupting, etc. However, such abuses can be inflicted by persons who are not narcissistic too. Anyone can inflict such abuses when angry. Before you label any of these verbal accusations narcissistic, consider the frequency of occurrence. You should also observe the emotions and reactions of the abuser during and after the abuse. Narcissists are not empathetic and draw satisfaction from abusing their victims. Even when they ask for forgiveness, they only do so to stop their victims from taking action.

Manipulation

Manipulation is another form of abuse that victims never realize. It occurs both during the early stages of friendship or relationship and also at advanced levels. During the early stages, manipulation occurs in the form of mental games. The narcissist uses trickery and claim to get someone to do something. As the two parties get acquainted, the narcissist slowly starts putting on the true colors. After fixing the victim in a corner, the narcissist will use any form of manipulation to get their way. Manipulation is often expressed in the form of aggression or threats. A narcissist behaves like a wolf; he/she uses aggression to scare the victim into doing things. In most cases, the victim may do things that seem mutual but deep inside they are not happy about it. It is very difficult for many people to spot manipulation, especially those who might have experienced manipulation while growing up.

Emotional Blackmail

Emotional abuses have the furthest reaching effects on narcissistic abuse victims. Emotional scars may take decades to heal and in some cases, may never heal. A narcissist inflicts emotional pain knowing that it will break down the victim. Emotional abuses are aimed at making an individual feel worthless. They provoke the feelings of doubt and eventually introduce low self-esteem in the victim. Emotional abuses are characterized by intimidation, shaming, threats, anger, warnings, or punishment. A person who is under emotional blackmail experiences anxiety, fear, and obligation. Such individuals are afraid of making any decisions or moves. They are terrified by the thought of the narcissist spotting them. A person who is under emotional blackmail always believes that the narcissist is watching. Even when they are alone, victims are afraid of making any attempt at escape because they believe the narcissist is omnipresent. They believe that they cannot run away from the abuser and eventually resign to the fact that the life they live is the only option they have.

Gaslighting

Narcissists enjoy when they control a person to the fullest. They use gaslighting to get into the victim's mind and make the victim distrust their perception of reality. They use words to make you think that they control your life. They will make a victim believe that the reality is worthless. They make victims believe that they are mentally incompetent and unworthy of living a normal life.

Unfair Competition

Narcissists have a desire to show superiority, and to achieve that, they use unfair games. They will introduce all forms of competition in life. They may compete with the victim socially, academically, financially, or in any way possible. They introduce competition to show the victim that he/she is worthless and does not match the status of the narcissist.

Negative Contrasting

Narcissists constantly use abuses to compare their victims to other people. They unfairly compare them to previous relationship partners or friends. In a family setting, narcissists compare siblings against others. They use the victim's weaknesses to make them feel worthless and undeserving.

Sabotage

Sabotage is another form of abuse inflicted a narcissist. They often target anything that makes the victim happy. They sabotage any activity, achievement or objective that might make the victim happy. They may sabotage academic success, break up relationships or terminate the victim's employment. The target of a narcissist is to end up having the victim doubting his/her abilities. Sabotage of the activities and achievements are a prime target for a narcissist, especially when dealing with self-reliable individuals.

Exploitation and Objectification

When you are in a narcissistic relationship, you eventually feel like an object. Exploitation entails using someone to fulfill personal goals. Narcissists constantly turn their victims into tools and objects. They use their victims to achieve anything they want in life. Sometimes, they may go to the extent of using their victims to commit crimes such as robbery. Once they have a person under control, they might use that person to steal or rob or do any job.

Pathological Lying

Continuous pathological lies are part of narcissist's true characters. Although many people may not consider laying an abuse, it inflicts serious pain on the victims. They lie in relationships, finances, family and all matters concerning their life. The first step to discovering anyone's identity is demanding to know the truth. When a person is a pathological liar, they fail to say the truth about their family history, upbringing, or even their job. An inquiry to find out such factors at the early stages of a relationship might help save an individual from narcissistic abuse.

CHAPTER 2

WHY DO NARCISSISTS ABUSE PEOPLE THEY LOVE?

One of the most outright difficult questions that you have to tackle when you decide to study something as dense and challenging as narcissism is the question of why people with narcissistic personality disorder abuse the people that they love. The trouble with narcissistic personality disorder is that it isn't as clear-cut as we would like for it to be.

For now, though, we're just going to try to get a clearer understanding of what is going on in the brain of somebody who is narcissistic, as well as analyzing what this information has to do with somebody's general behavior towards people that they love. This can be a bit of a difficult puzzle to piece together, so I ask that you bear with me as we try to make sense of this mess of a personality disorder.

The first thing that you need to understand about narcissistic personality disorder is that there is no singular cause. The cause appears to be a unified combination of things ranging from genetics to one's environment to one's upbringing. One also needs to understand that it doesn't seem to manifest in any singular uniform way. There are so many ways for narcissistic personality disorder to manifest, in fact, that psychologists and psychiatrists have determined up to eleven different subtypes of this disorder, all behaving in unique yet tangentially related ways.

We first need to establish that the basis of narcissistic personality disorder lies in the fact that a person not only desires but needs and thrives on the validation and acceptance of others. That is to say that a person who has narcissistic personality disorder feels that they must be accepted by others and seen as some image of greatness that they perceive themselves as.

In understanding this phenomenon, we can start to understand the concept of validation in narcissism a bit more. Mainly, we can use this as a jumping off point in order to start discussing why a person might behave like they do. The understanding of validation serves as an essential starting point to the understanding of why somebody with narcissism might abuse somebody that they love.

It's also important to note that not all narcissism is borne from the same reasoning. We discussed this bit a moment ago, but we're going to dive into it a bit deeper now: narcissism mainly has two root social causes. The first is that the person was under-praised, harshly criticized, or even suffered from some sort of emotional abuse as a child. In this case, the development of narcissistic personality disorder mainly served as a defense mechanism so that they wouldn't believe terrible things about themselves, acting as a method to block out the negativity and perhaps as a subconscious knee-jerk response to the emotional depth and vitriol they were forced to deal with.

The second cause is that the person was over-praised or otherwise validated in some central way by people who were important to them, such as parents or peers, without any sort of actual evidence in order to back up the level of praise that was rendered. This made the person in question feel exceptional while they were developing leading to them having grandiose visions of themselves and their abilities.

So, how does all of this play into somebody's patterns of abuse? Basically, with these two extremely different causes—causes which are, more or less, polar opposites. You need to understand that one way or another, the narcissist deeply craves validation from their partner or victim. It's unfortunate, but they really do thrive off of validation such that they subconsciously need it or else they will react in a knee-jerk way to the lack of validation, which often is rendered as emotional abuse, anger, general irritability, or either real or faux depression.

Another important thing to understand about the narcissistic patterns of abuse lies in the fact that narcissism is often comorbid with other extremely strenuous personality disorders. After all, most personality disorders have similar root causes as subconscious reactions in response to external stresses. These simultaneously acting personality disorders may be things such as borderline personality disorder or histrionic personality disorder, both of which serve to either end up with the extreme over- or undervaluation of partners and general figures in life, leading to an inevitably unsteady and often abusive relationship.

In understanding why people with narcissistic personality disorder choose to abuse their partners, it's also important to understand that many narcissists are only exhibiting learned behavior that they internalized as okay from a figure such as a father or a mother. Failure to realize behavior as unhealthy ultimately led to them accepting the behavior as a perfectly fine way to act. It, of course, is not a perfectly fine way to act, but the narcissist doesn't know any better and, at this point in their development, doesn't have the capacity to care either.

So really what I'm trying to say is that if a narcissist abuses their partner, there's a pretty decent chance that they themselves were abused by a narcissist in their lives. They then internalized this sort of behavior as acceptable and normal and then express themselves through that action in their own relationships. This isn't serving as a means to rationalize what they're doing or humanize them at all—abuse, in general, is absolutely grotesque and devastating. However, it does give one the ability to understand in a general sense why one might behave in the way that they do.

In the end, people serve one primary use to the narcissist: the validation of their own personality and the facade that they set up for themselves. A narcissist will find a person useful insofar as they are able to fulfill this purpose, and failure to fulfill this purpose will often lead to frustration on the narcissist's part.

The combination of the desire for intense validation and the need for admiration with the generally ingrained negative behavior patterns of the narcissist combines to create the perfect storm for a heavily unhealthy relationship based around validation, a lack thereof, and an incredible amount of underlying tension.

It's easy to ask the question: does the narcissist love me? While we are going to get into that question a bit more in-depth a little bit later, it's hard to answer on its own because the answer is a bit difficult to give. Understand that regardless of the narcissist's feelings for you, you ultimately simply serve as a part of their toolbox for self-validation.

However, this doesn't mean in and of itself that they don't or cannot love you. One thing you need to understand about narcissistic personality disorder is that despite the fact that they may feel capacity for love, the part of their brain which has to do with empathy is quite literally shrunken in most cases, which means that even if they can love, they don't feel the same amount of empathy that a neurotypical human being would. This can be a huge cause of stress in your relationship and lead to them not understanding why certain things that they do are fundamentally incorrect in a moral sense.

Do understand, though, that any extant love isn't a validation of the way that they may act towards you. There are a great many reasons that a narcissistic person may act abusively towards a person that they love. This does not, however, serve to make any of the reasons fundamentally correct or even relatively acceptable. They are not acceptable, flatly, and you ultimately deserve better than abuse—nobody deserves abuse.

It takes a lot of honesty with oneself to attempt to understand why somebody who has narcissistic personality disorder may choose to abuse the people that they love because it's immensely difficult to leave any sort of structure, especially if there's an abuse component to it. Your mind is actively working against you in these sorts of scenarios, so understanding that a person may be abusive and not the right sort of environment to be within is absolutely vital.

Manifestation of Narcissism

As you read on, you will learn of the various traits that are present in a pathologically narcissistic person. These are things that you will notice as you spend time with them and observe them. You cannot just look at a person and tell if he is narcissistic, at least in a pathological way. However, researchers have said that narcissism is actually quite visible in the physical appearance of some people. This manifestation of narcissism can be seen in the following ways:

They will wear expensive clothing and try to look flashy and great at all times.

They like being organized and looking neat. They invest a lot of time to prepare themselves and ensure this. You will never see them wearing a wrinkled shirt or a maybe a face without any makeup.

These are physical manifestations. The rest is seen in their behavior and actions, as you will learn. However, it is important to note that most narcissists are quite preoccupied with their outward appearance and want to look good all the time. They love being the center of attention and refuse to give anyone a chance to criticize them in any way.

CHAPTER 3

TIPS & TRICKS FOR RECOVERY

Although narcissistic abuse does have long-term effects, that doesn't mean that you will never be able to overcome those effects. The psychological and emotional wounds of narcissistic abuse will heal with time—as long as you give them the chance to do so. Even the effects of abuse on your brain can be reversed as you recover. Like a broken bone growing back stronger than before, you may even find that your new self is healthier and more resilient than the person you were before you suffered the abuse.

Waking Up

The first stage in healing is to understand how narcissistic personality disorder develops and what narcissism really means. Once you understand and accept this, a lot of things that seemed complicated and confusing should make a lot more sense. For example, you may have wondered how your partner could be so kind, loving, and attentive in some situations and so unpredictable, cruel, and undermining others. Now that you have a clearer understanding of narcissistic abuse, you know that there is really no contradiction at all. Both behaviors were merely expressions of your partner's underlying narcissism, which drives him to interact with others in a pattern that is much more predictable than you may have realized:

1. Idealization: in this phase, the narcissist projects all his fantasies about ideal love and support onto the new person in his life, giving them the false impression that he can heal their wounds and securing a new source of narcissistic supply.

2. Devaluation: in this phase, the narcissist projects all his inner fears, self-hatred, and insecurities onto the other person, destroying their sense of self. He may return to the idealization phase temporarily to keep his victim hooked but will always come back to the devaluation phase in a little while.

3. Discarding: in this phase, the narcissist finds someone else to provide him with narcissistic supply and discards the previous victim, often without warning.

Not many people will leave the narcissist in the idealization phase—it simply feels too good, especially for someone with unresolved childhood wounds. Generally speaking, only experts at spotting narcissists will recognize this stage for what it is and escape in time.

Many people will only leave once they are well into the devaluation phase and have already suffered a lot of damage. Many don't leave even then and are blind-sided when the narcissist leaves them for someone else. Either way, the first stage of healing is waking up: recognizing the narcissist for what he really is.

Highly empathic people are potentially vulnerable to narcissists for several reasons. One reason is that the childhood experiences that produce codependency also tend to produce children highly attentive to the emotions of the people around them. Another reason is the nature of empathy itself. If you're always the one who can see the other side of the story, if you're willing to meet people halfway, if you always want to understand and forgive, then you will find it much harder to face the harsh truth about the narcissist.

The narcissist's expressions of love might be convincing, but he is always in love with his own reflection. His remorse might seem genuine, but he is fundamentally incapable of loving other people in a healthy and mutually supportive way. His suffering is real, but his method of dealing with this suffering is to drain other people and then throw them away.

The gift of your empathy and understanding is wasted on the narcissist, who will only use it to keep you hooked while he systematically drains you of your sense of self. The sooner you start to think of the narcissist as a type of vampire, the sooner you will take the next step in the healing process: stepping out into the sunlight, where vampires cannot go.

Breaking Contact

Ending your relationship with the narcissist is an important step, but it will be hard to maintain unless you go all the way. Completely breaking contact is essential for healing because otherwise, the narcissist will do everything within his power to maintain control.

For example, if you move out of your abuser's house but stay in contact by phone, he will still have the ability to use almost every tactic in his manipulative repertoire. Even if you're determined not to go back to him, he can get a power thrill just by saying something he knows will push your buttons. The same is true if you remain in contact by email or if he keeps sending you messages through friends or family members. He may try to win you back with empty promises, or he may just try to hurt you or make you mad.

If you want to start healing as soon as possible, it's essential to break contact with the narcissist completely. Refuse to see him. Don't answer his phone calls. Delete his emails without reading them. Block his texts. Tell friends and family members who are still in contact with him that you aren't interested in getting any messages.

Along with breaking off all contact, resist the urge to check up on him or see how he's doing. Even glancing at his social media pages would be a mistake. One of the things he's most likely to do is to post pictures of himself having a great time with someone else to make you jealous, or ranting about how much you've mistreated him, or anything else he thinks might trigger an emotional reaction.

It's not easy to do this, but your goal should be not only to cut off all contact with the narcissistic abuser but to remove every last thread connecting their life to yours—including your thoughts.

If you do happen to run into the narcissist at a family event or in a public place, you can use something called the "gray rock" technique to keep them from regaining any of the power they used to have over you. As the name implies, the idea in this technique is to be like a wall of granite—flat and emotionless, not reacting to anything.

If you have children with a narcissist, you may not have any choice except to remain in contact with them. In this situation, the narcissist will probably try to retain as much emotional power over you as possible, perhaps for years.

To defend yourself from continued abuse in this situation, limit your contact to the bare minimum required by the court-ordered custody agreement. These agreements often allow you to specify the type and frequency of contact. For instance, you may be able to require your co-parent to call the children only at scheduled times or to refrain from contacting you except by email.

Some family courts can appoint a Guardian ad Litem to safeguard the legal interests of your children, or a Parent Coordinator to handle scheduling issues and any necessary communication.

Whatever the specific arrangements, make sure your custody agreement spells everything out in as much detail as possible and leaves no room for ambiguity.

Resist the urge to ask your children about your former partner, and never ask your children to carry messages for you. Even if it isn't easy to break off all contact, you need to get as close as possible to no-contact in order to heal.

Emotional Recovery - Steps to Heal

Go no contact. Rid yourself of the toxicity of the relationship. This will free your mind, so you can grieve, assess your situation, make life changes, heal, and grow as an individual. With the abusive narcissistic still lingering, it is difficult to get a clear head.

Acknowledge THIS WAS NOT YOUR FAULT. The narcissist's key tactic is for them to avoid and deviate from responsibility while dumping this on you. Take a sigh of relief and rest in this notion. You didn't cause this to happen, didn't deserve this to happen and do not merit being abused by a narcissist.

Take Responsibility – Step back and take a bird's eye view of your relationship. Were there red flags or did something that appeared off in the relationship? Think about this and assess.

Set up time with a professional counselor or therapist that specializes in narcissistic abuse. Make sure the counselor truly understands the situation. If any time, you feel the counselor is trying to place blame on you for the abuse, or if you feel the need to defend what happened and/or don't feel it's safe, find another counselor or therapist.

Realize your friends and family may not be supportive. Your friend and family may not be the ones you confide in and discuss the recovery. They just may not understand. As you search for validation, know this is the place where it may not be found.

Realize there are stages of grief and each stage takes time.

Take a break from social media. As your friends and family's lives are going on as normal and are posting their pics at the beach, and family vacation, and weekend events, it may be best to take a break from the lives people portray on social media. Use this time to take care of your emotional well-being and find another activity to engage in that will help your mind heal from the emotional rollercoaster you have been on.

Get a new pet. As you recover, a great new furry friend may be the best thing for you. Pets have a way of showing unconditional love to us.

Re-evaluate existing relationships. Do an inventory of your relationships and evaluate if there has been a pattern that attracted others into your life.

Resources: There are many resources available to assist on the internet. There are Facebook groups support for survivors, there are YouTube channels, and forums that can help to let you know you are not alone. Others have been there, and they can offer their support and encouragement.

Realize there will come a time when you are healed. The recovery process may take a while, and that is okay. Go through the stages.

Learn what it means to love and to value yourself

Get a massage or a facial. Get your nails or hair done. Buy a new pretty lipstick. Play golf with a buddy that you haven't seen in a long while.

Know that you are beautiful, fun and these qualities do not have to be broadcasted on Facebook for everyone to be aware of how special you are. Go through the process to receive inner peace with yourself and circumstances. Develop your new identity so that you are fully capable in your own skin even with the scars of the past. Know there is a quiet strength that can be birthed and it carries the qualities of gold in your inner being. You are a treasure to whom you choose to share your life with.

Establish your new identity. Learn new hobbies and activities, or take a trip.

Social Media

Many people post on social media their positive experiences only. Facebook may be coined Fake Book as it's not true reality. It's only a portion of the lives that people wish to share. During this time of emotional recovery, it may be best to limit time or take a break from social media. This may be difficult since we have been in a pattern that we are at fault for everything, we want to assert our side of the story. Unfortunately, this only makes things worse. Not only are we feeding the very thing the abuser wants and supplying them with narcissistic supply, but it does not solve the issues. A lot of strength and willpower may be needed to create and form new habits in response to the smear campaign that is launched. The wisdom is foresight that knowing it will be launched and knowing in advance how you will choose to react.

When dealing with the narcissist on social media platforms, this is different.

Block your narcissist abuser on all social media platforms. (Facebook, Instagram, LinkedIn, etc.)

Block your narcissistic abuser on your phone for text and email. Do not respond. Keep in mind the abuser will send flying monkeys to try and contact you.

As you heal, this is a time for inner development and restoration. I recommend you take a long break from Facebook and social media. It is reported that many everyday users report depression after using Facebook. As you are going through a unique healing time, use this time to take a break, a hiatus, for an extended time to cleanse your soul, restore your personality, create and re-establish new passions, enhance your vision for your future, weep, grieve, and have devoted time to yourself and your needs which have been neglected for so long.

It may be tempting to engage in conversation over social media regarding your narcissist ex or common friends. Resist the urge, disengage and take a mental break.

Do not respond to your narcissist abuser's emails. This enforces no contact.

Realize that the narcissistic abuser will send flying monkeys to you to question and will test your new boundaries. This may be difficult as some flying monkeys may also be your friends. This has to be evaluated closely to see their true intention.

CHAPTER 4

THE STAGES OF RECOVERY

To recover from narcissistic abuse and the childhood emotional neglect that often precedes it, we need to move away from the co-dependent behaviors that no longer serve us and learn new skills, one of which is to become 'self-approving'. When we're no longer relying on others to validate us, we begin to connect with our true Self and the recovery starts.

Stage 1 - Education

Learning about Narcissistic Personality Disorder (NPD), Co-dependency, Complex Post Traumatic Stress Disorder (C-PTSD), Childhood Emotional Abuse or Neglect, Grief and Trauma.

Stage 2 - Finding the Right Support.

Stage 3 - Narc Trouble Shooting - How to buffer yourself and offset the worst of their behavior.

Stage 4 - Finding out WHO you are.

Stage 5 - Life Long Learning - Healing and Moving Forward.

Children & Co-Parenting

This section raises the issues likely to arise when co-parenting with a narcissistic ex-partner and discusses how we can support our children through difficult times, help them build resilience and maintain their own 'Narc Buffers'.

But this frightening phase was a necessary evil - it's what I had to go through to get to the other side. I'd presumed these horrible feelings were about fearing Shaun's retaliation, but really it was about losing that connection. Toxic as it was, it was still a connection - I meant something to someone, I had a sense of belonging.

What Changes might we see when we Start to Recover?

A new feeling of independence may bring feelings of loneliness and disorientation, and although this is often uncomfortable, it's a sign that things are changing.

We find that our focus is moving inward and is no longer solely on the narcissist.

We start to feel brave and find we can stick up for ourselves without becoming emotionally dysregulated.

We begin to make healthier life and relationship choices and are less tolerant of fake or arrogant people.

We are aligning with those who share our same core values.

We have a greater understanding of why things are, the way they are.

We no longer experience drama, chaos and manipulation in our everyday life.

We're no longer hiding from anything or anyone - we know that to move forward we must work with our fears.

Our taste in men/women has changed.

We have stopped pretending to be someone we aren't, and we no longer play the chameleon.

We are taking more care of ourselves physically and emotionally and have begun to exercise self-compassion (not self-pity).

Mental Body speaks great truth, depending on whether or not we are ready to hear it. For example, it might say the reason we've stayed in a toxic relationship for so long is that we believe it's preferable to being alone. The Ego, which resides in Mental Body, often argues against any changes - it complains heavily about our situations but will not help resolve them because that means stepping out of known patterns and comfort zones. Mental Body struggles to gain control of the Ego and as a result, Ego often succeeds in calling the shots. Mental Body is known to mull over a situation for annoyingly long amounts of time, as it tries to make sense of something. A light bulb moment in the end may provide permanent relief, but if another 'Body' is needing attention, or Mental Body still hasn't quiet digested the message it needs to know, relief will be only temporary. Mental Body working alone is not able to heal the 'whole'.

Emotional Body often gets overlooked as Mental body exhausts itself trying to work things out. It's not easy to hear itself over the noise Ego makes as it judges, criticises and blames (Ego demands attention in the same way the narcissist does). Emotional Body doesn't judge - it just is, and because it works on a deeper level, the narcissist is deeply intimidated by it. He or she will feel the urge to minimise emotionally expressive people by saying such things as "Boo-hoo, here come the waterworks", or worse. They'll label a person weak, or weak-minded, but the accusation is often a projection of what's going on with them. Their own emotions were likely denied from a very young age, and they are reluctant to allow anyone else to have them either.

Narcissists don't want to be around emotional beings who remind them of who they are not. Their victims act as a mirror, reflecting their own emptiness, and watching someone express something they don't have is massively triggering. Anyone they perceive as being different can upset them to the point of lashing out with emotional or physical aggression. This prompts 'Shame', to attach itself to the narcissist's new victim - the cruel words have re-enforced old messages from their parents - something is wrong with them - no one is going to accept them - they are unlovable. Of course, the narcissist laps all this up and congratulates him or herself on the victory. But it was the victim's shame that disabled them, and not really the dirty work of the narcissist, so he can't really take the credit.

Emotional Body was likely suppressed by narcissistic parents repeatedly - in both the narcissist and the co-dependent. As the young child goes through the stages of development associated with becoming independent and forming their own unique identity, the narcissist mother or father halts it. She or he may have adapted to life with a baby thus far, but now that this child is starting to express their needs through emotion, the whole family thing is no longer going to work for this new parent. She must mold the child into something that is going to work for her - so she can get something out it.

The child is denied access to their own emotions, which are labelled bad, annoying, or selfish. Without realizing, the narcissistic mother describes herself with these words and projects what's going on with her, onto her child. This child now can't access the part of themselves that would typically guide a person towards emotional maturity, and a 'knowing' of who they are. The child develops new behaviors to avoid feeling this emotional pain and starts to hide their emotions, which pleases the mother and gives the child hope that one day, they will be accepted by her. But everyday life becomes a battleground for this child who is now living with unexpressed emotions stuck in their body.

Having had their emotions denied from a very young age, the adult-child has little idea who they really are and struggles to become self-reliant - they are a young child inside an adult's body. They're unable to recognize a healthy relationship from an unhealthy one and are treated in life, as they were in childhood. Often, they will turn to anything that helps numb the pain, and this is often alcohol, as it is legal, easy to find and socially acceptable.

The situation comes full circle when the adult child returns (or never leaves) the family home. The narcissistic mother shames and gossips about them for not growing up and taking responsibility for their life. Although the adult child is responsible for their own life, the mother was responsible for stunting the growth stages with emotional neglect and excessive control, of which the adult child is painfully aware. This harbors deep resentment and is further exacerbated by knowing that neglect and abuse will never be acknowledged. Despite all the complaining, the mother may enable her adult child by buying alcohol, drugs, or whatever they need, and won't encourage them to leave. The situation feeds her with narcissistic supply or serves her needs in some way - it may feed her martyr role, and the cycle of abuse continues.

In terms of healing the Emotional Body has much work to do, facing things that were always hidden, and daring to find out who it really is, is going to be difficult, but this essential act of self-kindness is do-able, at any age. With Mental and Emotional Body both working to support us, it may feel good, but is it enough? Somebody else is shouting - it's Physical Body protesting loudly, "This is all very well - being in touch with your thoughts and feelings, but my liver is turning to fat, and you put poison inside me every day, how can I support you if you keep doing this?"

You make a simple plan - with the help of someone else who can help motivate you, and you start becoming mindful of what you are putting into Physical Body. You now give it what it needs - proper nutrition, exercise and movement. Physical Body is powerful when it's in balance. As well as increasing energy in all areas, it also persuades Mental Body into producing extra 'feel good' feelings. Mental Body enjoys this immensely and can sometimes get hooked on this attention. If we are not careful, Physical and Mental Body will work together to numb the emotions and create an addiction - if the other Bodies are not also on board with this 'work-out'.

As Mental, Emotional and Physical Bodies start working together we notice that we seem to have more energy and self-control than before, and are now enjoying life on new levels, but…we're still having negative thoughts and wishing we had this or that. And we think, "Ugh, why do I feel something is missing, aren't I doing all I can already?" Not quite, Spiritual Body says, "I've been here all along and have watched everything. I want to tell you that I love you and you are not alone". You tear up or get 'truth bumps' as the core of who you are acknowledges this as being pure and honest.

Spiritual Body reminds you that you are a spiritual being, with a Higher Self that connects to whoever your God may be - and also the whole universe. When you realize (or remember) that we are all connected on a deeper level, the Ego takes a back seat, and a higher consciousness is felt in everyday life - this manifest as being more patient with others and not taking offence so easily. Once you feel this peace, the situations in your life seem more relaxed - you're not getting so wound up, and you're no longer being taken advantage of. You meet and attract others at this level, and it's around this time you learn about love - the love for yourself and love of others also. Now the healing journey has begun in earnest and won't be ending anytime soon because this will be a journey of a lifetime.

The person plagued with co-dependency issues can restore themselves, but it takes time, effort and commitment to find the person inside. We begin the recovery process by learning about co-dependency and narcissistic personality disorder, face up to what was done to us, and what we have unintentionally allowed others to do to us. We then learn how to offset the worst of the narcissist's behaviors (if we still need to be around one) and discover more about who we are as a person, what makes us tick, and what our goals and values are.

CHAPTER 5

THE AFTERMATH OF NARCISSISTIC ABUSE

There are several aftermath to narcissistic abuse. Most of them start during the relationship phase because even before you identify the problem, your body and mind recognize that something is not right and start exhibiting symptoms from the abuse. Abuse alters the way you think by entirely changing your perspective because you are no longer under your control but under the control of the abuser.

You may be wondering whether you are going mad or turning into a crazy person as the effects of the abuse lingers on long after the abuse has ended. Please understand that this is normal.

You are not going crazy, but it is your body and mind's way of dealing with the abuse that is inflicted upon. Hence, despite cutting off the relationship, healing takes time and a lot of patience.

During the healing journey, it is extremely important that you are kind and compassionate to yourself. Do not be critical of yourself and expect results overnight.

You may be wondering how long it will take? Well, the answer is that nobody knows how long it will take. While the relationship might have been for a short period, the healing takes a very long time. It also varies from person to person, so it is beneficial if you do not compare yourself to others and feel demotivated.

Brace yourself for the journey and continue reading to find out about the various effects of abuse and how to heal from it.

Anxiety

The stressful experiences victims are subjected to, often leads to anxiety, as the body naturally responds to stress that way. A constant feeling of fear of the unknown, the mind is in a perpetual state of panic as a way to defend itself, by forcing the person to flee that environment.

Anxiety happens when you live anywhere close to abuse. This can be due to mental, emotional, physical, or any abuse. This is because, in a relationship with a narcissist, you are constantly being put down and are being told that you are the cause of all troubles. Anxiety also happens in some cases because every time you summon the courage to report the abuse or confront the abuser, you are told that you are overreacting. Therefore, the brain does not understand how to handle all this, and thus, you have anxiety. Fear and anxiety are normal emotions everyone goes through at one point of the other, but when it never goes away and even gets worse with time, to the point where it starts to interfere with your day to day activities, you might be suffering from an anxiety disorder.

Anxiety may also cause you to experience panic attacks or panic disorders. These attacks lead to repeated episodes of intense anxiety. A narcissist manages to convince the whole world about their goodness because they are charmers, suave in their approach and extremely intelligent and guarded about their moves.

The first sign of your relationship with a narcissist is when you start feeling anxious for no specific reason. You start feeling trapped and begin to identify that something is wrong with your situation; however, the constant claims that the narcissist makes about your irrational behavior make you question yourself, and thus, you are lost and you develop anxiety.

Anxiety develops first because the brain is wired to respond to unhealthy behaviors. It is an evolutionary response to that is supposed to help you detect dangers and deal with those dangers.

In a way, the brain is telling you that something is wrong and that you have to make the wrong right.

So do not worry about the anxiety or panic attacks. It means that your body has identified threats and now you need to make things right.

PTSD

Post-traumatic stress disorder (PTSD) usually develops after the trauma of any kind. It is seen is army personnel who have served in wars to people who were involved in accidents to people like you who were abused.

If you have suffered from narcissistic abuse, it is common to experience constant flashbacks, almost like you are re-experiencing the entire trauma again. This can be very painful to deal with. Memories of trauma are involuntarily recalled despite you trying very hard not to recall them. This is because the memories are associated with trauma and can be caused by anything in the environment that resembles the event when the actual trauma occurred. The intrusive memories are extremely clear, making you feel like you are experiencing it all over again. You experience extreme fear because you feel like you are reliving the trauma.

These flashbacks are unique to PTSD, and these can also occur in the form of nightmares and cause tremendous fear in you. The nightmares are usually threatening or frightening dreams that awaken you and are followed by an intense negative emotion such as anger, fear, or sadness. You may experience body pains and muscle aches when you get up from your dream suddenly and find yourself often breaking down, unable to handle the emotional turmoil.

This is because unlike regular nightmares that you may experience, post-trauma nightmares are exceptionally intense as they contain the exact replay of the events that happened. These are called as replicative nightmares, where the dream plays out exactly the way it happened in real life, and you end up feeling like it is happening all over again and become helpless.

Flashback is also common where you may catch yourself during the day reliving those memories from the past. It is these intrusive thoughts and memories that lead to stress.

In some cases, these replicative dreams may persist even decades after the trauma has happened.

Apart from the above most common sign of PTSD, below are some other signs:

Physical Numbness

This can be anywhere in the body, right from toes, lips, muscles, etc., to emotional numbness (i.e., the inability to feel any emotion, especially unable to find joy in things that would otherwise bring joy to a normal person).

Memory Loss

You may be wondering how you remember and get nightmares about the abuse but tend to have forgotten a lot of other things. You cannot recollect certain parts of your life no matter how hard you try.

Fight-or-Flight Response

Your body is constantly on alert, and the slightest feeling of threat can send you into a fight or flight mode which means that either you are angry and want to fight or you want to escape.

PTSD happens because when you are exposed to narcissistic abuse, you are trapped, and your inner being is ripped apart. This is almost similar to living in a war zone.

The good news is that there is help around. You can seek help by consulting psychologists who are trained in this.

Depression

It is a very well-known fact that a breakup with a narcissist and even a relationship with a narcissist is extremely painful. Pain circuit within your brain is activated during this time. This feeling offsets your emotions, and you begin questioning everything. All this questioning leads to "Why me?"

When you start questioning "Why me?" you tend to become angry and upset that you were cheated and betrayed. This can lead you to think that you must have done something wrong or that you were unworthy of a good relationship. All these negative emotions can lead to low self-esteem and eventually to depression.

A narcissist thrives on making you lose your self-esteem and wants to tear you apart because only that will make them feel good. They will put in a lot of effort to ensure that this happens. Hence, when you understand this background, it is only natural that you expect an apology.

An apology never happens, and if it happens, it is never true. Even here your expectations are not met, and you go down the negative road. All this leads to depression simply because of the helplessness, betrayal, and the cheating you have experienced.

The fear that you are crazy can make depression worse. Depressive episodes usually peak as soon as you get up in the morning and open your eyes. It does not matter that you have still not gotten out of bed, but you already feel a lump in your throat and sometimes can even break down immediately.

Sleeplessness and Loneliness

All the nightmares and terrors make a seemingly easy task like sleeping seem like conquering the Mount Everest. It becomes impossible to catch even a few hours of sleep because no sooner do you close your eyes, you are bombarded with nightmares and traumatic feelings. Despite the constant fatigue, sleep eludes you. Depression adds to the woes by making it even worse. Feelings of loneliness and vulnerability are heightened at night and ensure that you do not sleep.

All the negative emotions and lack of self-esteem followed by social anxiety can make you want to avoid any social setting, thus making you prone to loneliness, even during the day.

Loneliness is also present because the narcissist would have cleverly isolated you from any human being he perceives as a threat or thinks will support you. It is extremely common for victims of narcissistic abuse to have lost all friends and contact with even close family members because that is just how the narcissist works. The narcissist would have enjoyed that you cut off the relations with everyone so now when you need any form of support you are left with none. All these feelings can worsen the depressive episodes.

Tiredness

If you're drowning in the aftermath of the narcissistic abuse, you will soon realize that you feel older than your age and generally exhausted.

Your muscles become stiff, you constantly feel tired and overwhelmed, and your joints are always in pain. This is because living with a narcissist is like living inside a volcano; you never know when he will explode. All the constant stress weakens your system because there is only so much stress the human body can handle. No matter how strong you are, there comes a crumbling time when your body gives up. It begins to stop cooperating, and that is when all these symptoms show up.

Exposure to constant abuse transforms your body into a state of fight or flight. When your body is in a state of fight or flight, its natural response is to produce cortisol. Cortisol is a hormone that is produced by the body when it is under extreme duress. When you are stressed, the amount of cortisol increases as your body has to manage increased levels of stress. Over some time, your body cannot deal with the stress anymore, and this is when you start feeling exhausted and tired all the time. A narcissist destroys both your body and mind at the same time.

Narcissistic abuse is difficult to spot initially because a narcissist is rarely overt, especially in the initial days. The abuse is silent and subdued, and because of which, you fail to recognize it. A narcissist will rarely indulge in physical abuse, and this makes things all the more difficult for you to process because you and society, in general, are conditioned to believe that if there are no bruises, then there is no abuse.

You are stressed because of both the abuse as well as trying to make sense of the extreme highs and lows in your relationship. All this stress starts showing up as soon as the stressor (i.e., the narcissist is removed from your life). Your body senses that the threat is no longer there and starts relaxing. This is when you begin processing all that has happened to you and experience nightmares and flashbacks.

Exposure to abuse causes this kind of adrenal fatigue because the primary function of the adrenal glands is to help deal with stress. Hence, during your relationship with the narcissist, your adrenal glands are working overtime beyond their capacity to help you deal with the stress and trauma that is being inflicted on you. Now with the abuser gone, the stressor is removed, and hence, you have fatigue. This is made worse by the fact that you are suffering from sleeplessness and depression. The constant nightmares keep you awake all night, and this, in turn, causes fatigue.

CHAPTER 6

GETTING AWAY FROM THE NARCISSIST

Narcissistic Injury and Narcissistic Rage

The hardest battle you will fight is not one for your recovery. It's the fight for your right to leave the narcissist. Creating physical, mental and emotional distance between you and the narcissist are crucial aspects of the recovery process. They will never make it easy, and getting away from them may be a very traumatizing experience - especially when you don't know what you're dealing with. Unfortunately, there is no easy way out and we have to face the narcissist in their injured and enraged state if we wish to be free.

Depending on the type of your relationship with the narcissist and the degree of their dependency on you at the point of your decision making, they may completely ignore your efforts to leave them at first. For example, if your parent is a narcissist and you begin looking for an apartment – they won't be concerned until you actually bring the news that you found a great place and are about to sign the contract. However, if your partner is a narcissist and you have a child together, you can expect them to blow up right away. In either case, the narcissist will tell a different story to others when it comes to your decision to leave them. Their story may change according to their mood, too. For instance, they may tell your friends that you've decided to leave and act as if they don't care about it. Then, they will tell their friends that they have dumped you. Your parents may get to know how hurt and sad the narcissist is about your decision to go etc.

In the end, it really doesn't matter whether they are your parent, roommate or partner. The narcissist's reaction to your decision to distance yourself from them will always be somewhat predictable. Their favorite tool is fear. The narcissist will usually make you fear and doubt your decision to leave them in one way or another. Their methods really depend on how high up on the narcissistic spectrum they are.

Narcissistic injury will get triggered the very moment they realize that yes, you are indeed leaving them. This is so, because anything that threatens the narcissist's status or projected ego, a.k.a. False Self, is bound to result in narcissistic injury. And when their response is disproportionate in comparison with the situation at hand, we call it narcissistic rage. Your choice to distance yourself from the narcissist is and never was a part of their projection. As soon as you decide to take initiative and leave, they get confronted with the fact that they simply cannot control all of your actions. Their reaction will be swift, irrational, confusing and nerve-racking – but only if you didn't see it coming!

Normally, the injured narcissist will attempt to beat you back into submission through emotional manipulation. With you about to leave, beating you back into submission may no longer be an option, so the narcissist would likely throw a tantrum. They may even yell that you've completely lost it – yes, you're insane to think that you can just leave like that! (Look who's talking, right?) It's not uncommon for them to say that you've got nowhere to go and lose their temper once they realize that, in fact, you do have somewhere to go. The raging narcissist will likely resort to threats or physical abuse on top of everything. You know them best, make sure to stay safe around them.

If you're lucky, however, they'll simply talk negatively about your plans all the time and express their doubts that you're going to make it on your own – either by scoffing at you while you prepare to go or by leaving passive-aggressive, toxic remarks. "That money of yours isn't going to last long", "I really hope your dream won't turn into a nightmare", "We'll see how well you'll do" - they're quick to tell you that you're not ready to leave and be on your own, and they love to question your decision in a way that is supposed to invoke fear and doubts in your mind. "Why are you going so far away? You'll be all on your own!", "You're just trying to run away from problems", "If you want to make it out there, you must learn to deal with real problems first – and you'll face many real issues once you leave, you can't even imagine it yet. I'm just trying to make you understand what's coming"

The narcissist will deny that they are trying to deter you from leaving, of course. If you ask them, they'll say that they are being "realistic" and that they are talking from experience. Don't let their narcissistic injury stop you from doing what's best for you. There's absolutely no way around it – you must find a way to distance yourself form the narcissist in order to heal.

It's not always easy

Sometimes, we won't be able to completely escape from the narcissist though. Maybe your parent is a narcissist and you don't have the financial means to leave their home right away. Perhaps your spouse is a narcissist, and you share custody of your child or children. Maybe the narcissist is the roommate you depend on financially, and there seem to be no other options for you at the moment. What we have to remember, however, is that there is always an option. For instance, should you lack financial means, you can look for ways to make money online (e.g. through online language teaching, offering services on fiverr, or by becoming a social media assistant etc). You could also seek help from those who you are close with – someone who can support you through difficult times.

It may take time until you can break away from the narcissist, but there is always going to be a way out. Most of the time, the narcissist is the one who put the idea that you're unable to escape in your head, in the first place. His or her world depends on you, how dare you think you can just leave?

Sometimes, we'll have to stay in touch with the narcissist even after we physically get away from them. It's important to know that the narcissist will always continue to criticize everything about us, involving our new environment. You got a new apartment? Of course, it's not as great the narcissist's last own place, but don't worry, they surely know that you can get something better soon! You got a new job? Honey, you should spend your summer holiday somewhere nice this year, because you'll have it tough while climbing the career ladder in the coming years all on your own! You got a roommate or partner? Ah, that's why you sound upset all the time, things aren't going well at home, are they? What? You changed your eating habits? You must take better care of yourself; you look so pale and thin now!

You get the idea. The moment you leave the narcissist, but have to keep in touch with them for whatever reason, your life will be under inspection. The narcissist will be quick to assume details about your private life and paint a dirty picture. If you fall for this trick, they'll have you hooked and you'll continue to be their narcissistic supply. Your attempts to correct their wrong assumptions will make them feel superior and will only lead to more negative comments. I suggest that, if you absolutely have to stay in touch with the narcissist, you should keep the contact to a minimum. Never share any negative or even slightly negative news with them. Cut the conversations down to meaningless small talk and only speak about good things that happened to you. This will leave the narcissist little opportunity to drag you down and you will have an easier time focusing on your recovery.

The situation is that, in their mind, your real life does not exist. They don't care about reality. Your personality, emotions, goals and aspirations don't exist to the narcissist. The narcissist sees you through a filter – they decide what you are, how you think, how you feel and how you live, with or without them. There's absolutely nothing you can do to prove them that you are doing good and that you don't need them to be well off. If the narcissist wants to believe that you are doing terribly on your own, they will act as if you are. It is very dangerous, because as a healthy individual, you will still consider their perspective to be valid. If the narcissist keeps telling you that your talk sounds so negative all the time, you may believe that you truly sound toxic, and that you're really not doing well in life. You may begin to criticize your decisions and see yourself as a failure.

There is real danger to believe that you've become the failure the narcissist pictures you to be without them. This is because years of emotional manipulation and broken self-esteem don't get undone just by physical distance alone. A part of you believes the narcissist, no matter how far away you are, no matter how little contact you have with them. And even if the narcissist never gets the chance to criticize your life ever again, their internalized voice will initially do it for them in your mind.

There's also the possibility that your narcissist will completely discard you once you leave. Your self-doubts will pull you towards thoughts about the narcissist and you may even feel guilty for ending your relationship with them. If that happens, remind yourself that it is the voice of the narcissist in your head, telling you that you've done a terrible mistake. If you are over the age of 18, you are legally free to do whatever you want with your life and leave whomever you want. There is absolutely no reason for you not to work towards a better future. You must also understand that whatever little contact you'll still have with the narcissist from time to time will always be negative and worrisome in nature. That's because it's how narcissists work. You will still have a lot of healing to do in order to overwrite the distorted self-image forced on you by the narcissist and you should be prepared for that.

When you have broken away from them, you might become depressed or frustrated over how you still can't stop thinking about them. They'll run through your mind, and you'll worry about how they're doing and whether you have caused them lots of pain. There may be many things you'll wish to tell them. This is just because you have been conditioned by the narcissist to prioritize them in life. You have been looking at yourself through their distorted perception of you and you've become accustomed to it. The truth is, you only have this mentality because they put it in your mind in the first place. All these negative thoughts and beliefs about yourself are not truly your own.

No matter what you're going through once you distance yourself from the narcissist, I want you to know that it's okay to worry about what they think. Maybe they pop into your head when you're trying on clothes in the dressing room, or when you say something embarrassing in a conversation - they're the voice in your head that told you that you sounded stupid. Remember that this is just because they were able to get and control you in the first place. It doesn't indicate whatsoever that those thoughts are right and that they belong to you from now on. You have a choice between letting these thoughts define you as a person or giving yourself the permission to define yourself. It's okay to change, you know? Our goal is to learn to recognize the internalized voice of the narcissist whenever it comes up. We'll be able to overwrite it with our own thoughts soon enough!

The narcissist has done plenty of work to make sure that they have control over your life, so their nagging voice will not go away overnight. The narcissistic abuse might have lasted a few years, or perhaps even decades. No matter the length, it will take time to heal the damage and fully recover from the abuse, but it doesn't have to take years or decades to overcome it! Though there is no magic pill to cure the trauma, always keep in mind that it is possible to heal – and do so quickly - as long as you take action and focus on your goal.

CHAPTER 7

DISTINGUISHING NARCISSISM

FROM OTHER PERSONALITY DISORDERS

Narcissistic personality disorder or NPD falls on a spectrum of personality disorders that can cause a great dysfunction to those suffering from them and great suffering to those around them. NPD represents a pervasive pattern of behaviors that those dealing with the narcissist are likely familiar with, although this can also be said of the other personality disorders that narcissistic personality disorder is grouped with and sometimes mistaken for.

For those trying to overcome narcissistic abuse, the differences between the disorders may be minimal. Emotional abuse, whatever its source, can leave the target feeling exhausted, emotionally drained, and vulnerable. Indeed, one of the goals of narcissistic abuse is to leave the target in a dependent, weakened state, which not only keeps the target close to the narcissist—which the narcissist wants—but also leaves the victim open for continued abuse.

Remember that the narcissist may not care about the emotions of others, but he or she is generally aware of them. This awareness that the narcissist has of the emotions of the individual they are abusing is part of what can make narcissistic personality disorder hard to understand and painful for the abused. This is a characteristic of a personality disorder in general. They can be difficult to understand because the way that the person with the disorder thinks is generally so different from how others think. The narcissists themselves can feel a superiority to others and can have difficulty relating to other people at the same time.

Other Personality Disorders that Can Affect a Relationship

These disorders also can seriously impact a relationship and result in emotional abuse. A borderline personality disorder is divided into a borderline type and an impulsive type, both of which experience significant emotional disturbances that can lead to emotional abuse in a relationship. Borderlines tend to be more dangerous to themselves than they are to their partners, making the problems that the partner of the borderline person faces more secondary to their dysfunction than deliberate as is the case with the narcissist.

Histrionic personality disorder bears some similarities to borderline personality disorder, particularly in the interactions that the histrionic person has with those around them. Histrionic personality disorder refers to a type of personality characterized by excessive emotionality, attention-craving behaviors, seductive behaviors and inappropriateness, and an excessive need for approval. Indeed, the histrionic person has some of the traits that have been assumed by the narcissist in film. Histrionic personality is interesting in that its relationship to narcissism is clear, although these individuals tend to be more difficult than abusive in relationships.

Antisocial personality disorder has distinctions from the term antisocial that is in common parlance in conversation. Antisocial is often used to refer to people who lack interest in forming relationships with others or who lack social skills. But antisocial personality disorder specifically refers to individuals who have an oppositional or adversarial view of society or other people and who engage in criminal or other destructive acts. These individuals are dangerous but in a different manner from the narcissist, as their traits may be more obvious to those around them, and therefore, potential partners are less likely to be unwittingly manipulated as they would be by a narcissist, for example. Antisocial personality disorder sits on the other side of NPD compared to histrionic personality disorder, representing perhaps the more destructive, dark psychological aspects of narcissism.

It is important to spend a moment examining the subject of dark psychology as it relates to how narcissism is connected with other conditions. Again, though Freudian theories may be superficially discredited in modern psychology, the legacy of Freudian thinking is obvious in the tendency to view psychiatric conditions, particularly personality disorders, in terms of the drives of the id. Leaving aside the issue of libido, what these conditions have in common is a type of self-interest or normal infantile narcissism that leads the individual with the personality disorder to always see their own needs as paramount to others.

In the case of histrionic and borderline individuals, this can lead to excessive emotionality, attention-seeking behaviors, and other actions designed to fulfill a deep emotional need for attention. Borderline individuals are known for sending mixed messages of love and hate, which are related more to their own disordered emotional states than a desire to manipulate or harm other people. Borderline traits most likely have a different origin from narcissistic traits, despite some of the similarities. Some borderline individuals have a history of abuse or neglect, which can lead them to have distorted subconscious perceptions of love and hate and a need for validation by others.

Borderline and histrionic personality disorders, therefore, stray from the dark energy associated with narcissistic personality disorder and antisocial personality disorder. Indeed, individuals with antisocial personality disorders may be motivated to engage in destructive behaviors because they hate society or other people or because they have intense feelings of anger or for no reason at all. Committing harmful acts without a clear motivation or goal is one of the core concepts of dark psychology, as the behaviors in this latter category can involve individuals tapping into a reservoir of negative, destructive energy that has no clear purpose.

This is an area of dark psychology that is actively explored in that field but relatively ignored in formal psychology. Indeed, modern psychological theory draws much from Alfred Adler's individual psychology theory and sees human actions as having purposive motivations. But in dark psychology, there is an admission that human beings can commit wanton acts of violence that have no benefit, a characteristic that is not seen in other species in the animal kingdom. This capacity to behave with wanton destruction is key to understanding dark psychological concepts, and the narcissist is one of the character types that this burgeoning field explores.

It can be difficult for the sheltered person to understand truly what we mean by dark or negative energy, but this represents a type of driving force that appears to be unrelated to any known motivation, even a libidinous one. Sigmund Freud tended to associate motivations that he perceived as primal or irrational (in contrast to the superego) with libido, possibly because of a subconscious assumption on his part that negative actions committed by men and women probably have to do with sex drive. In fact, as we have seen with the other cluster B personality disorders, the drives of men and women with dysfunctional personality traits can frequently have nothing to do with sex and rather represent a primal, human quality that has not been well-described in psychology.

Narcissism as a personality trait sits alongside two other types in a cluster that some psychologists have labeled the dark triad. The dark triad does not have a formal place in psychiatric practice the way that cluster B personality disorders do, but they represent a desire to understand the types of personality traits that can be particularly dangerous for others to deal with. Existing alongside narcissism is Machiavellianism and Psychopathy. Machiavellianism is a type of antisocial personality trait or cluster of traits, that is associated with the writings of Niccolo Machiavelli. Individuals displaying this type of behavior are willing to use any means necessary to obtain their ends, being motivated more by a misguided desire to accomplish a goal than by the vanity of the narcissist.

What it is important for the target of narcissistic abuse to know is that Machiavellian individuals can also engage in emotional abuse but would generally lack the codependency characteristics of the narcissist (unless they also have a narcissistic personality disorder). The Machiavellian abuses and manipulates because they see this behavior necessary for them to achieve their goals and because they perceive the lives and well-being of others as less important than their own if not entirely insignificant.

Because of behavioral similarities between the narcissist and the Machiavellian type, tips on protecting oneself from the narcissist would also apply to Machiavellians. Although their motivations might be different, learning to understand the emotional turmoil and manipulation that they direct against others, especially in relationships, will represent the first step in defending against this behavior. It does help to understand that the narcissist belittles others because they want to enhance their self-image and to keep the other person close to them. Though the Machiavellian may not be motivated by the same degree of vanity, defending oneself from this behavior by distancing from the perpetrator or learning to doubt and question the perceptions inherent in the words of the person saying them, would apply to both narcissists and Machiavellians.

Indeed, as the reader will see later, having a little bit of normal adult narcissism actually goes a long way in dealing with individuals with personality disorders or dark triad personality types. Normal adult narcissism in this context would mean that you understand your self-worth and would, therefore, doubt words from the narcissist that imply that you have low worth. Individuals who are used to narcissistic abuse can see their normal adult narcissism totally obliterated as the relationship only leaves room for one person to have confidence and self-esteem.

Psychopaths represent a behavior type that goes beyond what even psychiatrists can handle. In fact, the real value of understanding these dark triad and cluster B personality disorders is in immediately alerting others that they need to be extremely wary of these people. The psychopathic person is somewhat different from the narcissist in that they will lack the charm that allows the narcissist to insinuate themselves into your psyche. You give the narcissist the ability to control you because they have used their words to manipulate and seduce you and because they have recognized your weaknesses and exploited them.

Think about it this way. When the narcissist sharply devalues your appearance or states outright that you are attractive, they are actually saying that you are lucky to have them and implying that their own attractiveness is superior to yours. What this type of mental abuse does is satisfy their own vanity by placing them on a perch higher than you, and it also fulfills the narcissist's need for validation because when you tolerate this type of behavior, you basically agree that the narcissist is correct in their belief that they are better than you.

But the psychopath is different, as their behavior can be so destructive and outrageous that someone involved with them romantically would be the most unobservant person in the world if they did not notice that something is wrong. Both the psychopath and Machiavellian types are more noticeable to others because their beliefs and behaviors represent a greater divergence from normal behavior than the narcissist. The narcissist is so stealthy because they know just how to construct their image such that you do not notice that there is something wrong with them. The distinctions between NPD and some of these other personalities will become more apparent as the subject is explored further.

CHAPTER 8

NARCISSISTIC STRATEGIES OF MANIPULATION

It is one thing to understand manipulation, and how it works and can wreak havoc on your life. Understanding all the different tricks and tactics that a manipulator can use against you. May make it seem like it is impossible to defend yourself against manipulation. But the truth is that by understanding in excellent detail how manipulators can use a wide array of tactics against you. You use their weapons against them, something they are not expecting. To understand a potential enemy and the tactics they might use is to beat them at their own game. Too often manipulators enter our lives because we find their companionship pleasing, we let them fill a need that they create. This need can come from many places, for some a broken home, for others a simple need for action. To not know yourself is the greatest asset a manipulator can use against you. They act like parasites burrowing their way into your life and sucking you dry, getting all that they can resource-wise and then leaving you.

The good news is that you can avoid having this happen to you if you don't let it. Too often we let people dictate how they can treat us by our actions. If we let someone convince us that we are weak and need them to succeed than is it their fault for us getting sucked into their web. Or is it perhaps our fault for convincing ourselves that this "relationship" is good for us. The truth of the matter is that manipulators like to prey on people who have been hurt before. Their charm, and glib cons us into thinking that they will help us with whatever issue we are dealing with. It may sound cold or blunt but by keeping your guard and check and not letting yourself get too close to someone upon meeting them you can quickly avert any potential mishaps or crisis that may come forward within that relationship.

I would also like you to consider that for some individuals their manipulation is pathologic, meaning that there is some underlying mental illness that is causing them to behave this way. These types of people are the most dangerous for the simple fact that they do not realize that they are doing anything wrong, Think of your sociopaths or bipolar. For others their tendencies for manipulation can be linked to a faulty maturation process, they think that it will always be their way or the highway. In the end, the motivations remain the same for all manipulators when boiled down and simplified, they want what they want, and they are going to get it by whatever means it takes.

Being confident is your first step in averting a manipulative attack, depending on the type of manipulation used you are going to want to be confident in different areas. The manipulation that a salesperson might use varies greatly than the type of manipulation a jaded lover would use on you, so knowing how to respond to each is paramount. For example, if you know a car is cheaper than someone is saying is be firm in your argument and do not let up ground. The same can be said if you suspect your partner of lying in a romantic relationship. By showing dominance in an encounter you say to the manipulator that you are not someone who will fall for their bait, you will not be their plaything. Moving on from just simply being confident and knowing your situation, there is de-escalation. Many manipulators when confronted about their behavior like to make the stakes of a situation seem higher than they are. With their end goal being that you will back off and drop the conflict out of fear.

Their goal is to scare you into submission, through whatever means required. Some will threaten suicide, some will threaten you directly, in the hopes you will back down. The trick here is to call their bluff and remain firm in your conviction that you know they are just trying to manipulate you.

Do not buy into their bluffs as once a manipulator realizes they can get away with something once they will do it again and again. As you set a precedent for them that manipulative behavior is okay. Calling a manipulators bluff in a high-tension scenario like this, in the beginning, may lead to them getting irater and more irrational. But if you are firm and stand your ground, they will quickly come to terms with the fact that they will not win here. The other component of de-escalation is not losing control of your own emotions, manipulators are very good at learning what buttons to press to set you off. Understand this when interacting with them, because if you just buy-in and get as angry and irrational as them then you are stooping to their level and letting them get what they want from you, which is usually attention. There are some simple calming techniques you can use when you feel your emotions brewing up. Take a slow deep breath and count to five in your head, you can also try peaceful imaging. Imagine yourself on a calm beach or somewhere pleasant to draw your mind away from the situation with the manipulator. Presenting yourself as calm shows a potential manipulator that you won't stoop to their level and are willing to not compromise your integrity. De-escalation tricks are pointless if you do not take active steps to change things from there, this can be as simple as trying to set firm boundaries. The way you do this is that you let someone know what your limits are what you won't put up with, for example, if someone lies to you and you catch them you are firm and consistent with the consequences of it. If establishing boundaries and trying to de-escalate the situation don't work, then it may perhaps be in your best interest to reduce the amount of contact you have with the manipulator.

Going low or no contact with a manipulator guarantees you that they cannot harm you. The problem with doing this is remaining firm in your conviction, it is very easy to tell someone that you are going to stop contacting them but doing it is much more challenging.

Once a manipulator feels you are pulling away, they will ramp up their scheming in the hopes they can entice you into staying with them. Simply put leave them to block their number and possible leave any friends you both shares. Manipulators love to use other people to do their bidding. This allows them to act through proxies and avoid arousing suspicion that they are the ones responsible for certain behaviors. You may find that the more challenging part of reducing contact with someone who is a manipulator is the obstacles you set yourself. Manipulators like to make you second guess yourself and doubt your instinct in the hopes that you will follow through with their intentions. This is why knowing certainly how you want to act is important. Take time to do your diligence before making any major decision pull back for a little bit and analyze all the facts at your disposal.

By taking a calm and measured approach to your decisions and actions you present an image of someone who is not weak. This more than anything will prevent you from becoming a victim of manipulators attacks. Because it represents the image that you are in control of their emotions and as a result can't have your own emotions used against you, as manipulators commonly try to get you to do. In closing know that you have a basic understanding of some of the methods manipulators use and how to defend yourself against them. You are now better able to understand where manipulation truly comes from and what drives people to use someone's own emotions against them. As a result of knowing how their weapons work you can utilize them in tricky situations in life, where they may prove incredibly useful. Because manipulation is so common in today's fast-paced world it is imperative for you to understand it if you want to get ahead. That is why I would like to discuss how psychological disorders play in manipulative behavior. Since these personality disorders present themselves as continues displays of abhorrent behavior it is easy to recognize them when you know the signs. The three most common disorders that make people prone to manipulative behavior are Antisocial Personality Disorder (APD), Narcissistic Personality Disorder (NPD), and Borderline Personality Disorder (BPD). Understanding the pathologies and behaviors characterized by these kinds of psychological disorders allows you to quickly weed out people who could potentially be manipulators. While it may seem cruel to avoid someone because they have a "disorder" when it comes to your wellbeing and security you can never be too careful.

To begin the conversation on disorders that make one manipulative I would like to start with the lesser-known Borderline Personality Disorder or BPD. BPD as a disorder is characterized by an intense pattern of instability in both interpersonal relationships and sense of self, this instability is accompanied by an extreme of abandonment, when combined with the general impulsiveness and mood swings BPD brings make for a perfect storm of destructive behavior. Since individuals with BPD have such an intense fear of abandonment they may lie and manipulate to keep you closer to them while at the same time getting angry at you for spending so much time with them. This splitting between their desires and fears is where the term borderline comes from, their emotions are always bordering on the edge. Ever so close to teetering off and having a nuclear meltdown but still so far away. Often people with borderline personality disorder present their symptoms in a chaotic or disorganized fashion, which reflects the fact that they are unsure of who they are themselves. It is not known what causes an individual to develop a borderline personality disorder, but it is theorized that growing up in an abusive home or experiencing severe trauma at a young age makes someone more likely to develop it. An individual with Borderline personality disorder may be able to lure you in with how they may appear to make themselves vulnerable.

They are prone to sharing intimate details with their life very early on in a relationship in the hope of establishing trust and moving the relationship along quickly.

This where the instability in relationships comes to play, a person with a borderline personality disorder will want to move a romance or relationship much quicker than it should be. Their reasoning for this is their fear of being abandoned, this fear drives their whole being to such an extent that they will burn all their bridges in the ill-guided hope of keeping you. One of the final characterizations of BPD is a repeated pattern of intense tantrums and meltdowns when people leave them, for lack of a better word when this fear of abandonment ends up coming true due to self-sabotage borderlines have a bad tendency to self-destruct and burn down everything in their path.

Your best defense against a borderline is leaving before you are too involved. If someone wants to move a relationship quickly in a direction you don't feel comfortable with then it is in your best interest to leave while you can and when you have not invested much emotion. Moving on from one of the least known disorders, I would like to discuss a disorder we have all heard of Narcissistic Personality Disorder or NPD.

NPD is characterized by extreme self-centeredness and an inability to comprehend and understand the consequences of their actions. Because of this inability to understand consequence narcissists tend to repeat the same self-destructive behavior over and over again. We have all heard this term used to describe someone. Few of us actually understand what narcissism truly looks like. We are quick to label any behavior we don't like as narcissism when in reality it is subtler than that. Narcissists are not the overt self-centered people the media likes to portray them as. A narcissist likes to utilize subtle tactics to get you to come in line with their way of thinking, as opposed to overt manipulation. By getting you to question your judgment they can replace your ideas with theirs. One of the main behaviors all narcissists follow is the inability to take responsibility for their actions.

They will pin the blame for their actions on others instead of realizing that they are the reason misfortune keeps befalling them. As a result of this inability to learn from past mistakes, the narcissist will often repeat the same behavior over and over again to try and meet the same goal. This is what makes them so dangerous, they are willing to go to extreme measures to get their goals. The largest danger from narcissists comes from what is called a narcissistic meltdown. When a narcissist feels cornered like an animal, they will meltdown and destroy everything in their path even if it means damaging themselves. This can take many different forms, for some narcissists, this means something as extreme as suicide or even murder. For others, they may trash a lover's house when asked to leave the relationship. In short, when a narcissist realizes their game is up, they tend to blow a lot of fuses in their heads.

It is hard to postulate what motivates a narcissist as to behave this way current psychological research, points to a poor sense of self. But the truth is it does not matter why they do something that matters is your ability to avoid it. Narcissistic manipulation mainly takes the form of what is called gaslighting. Which in simple terms is the act of getting you to question your judgment of a situation and get you to think that you're the one with the issues and not them? By getting you to question your own beliefs regarding their behavior a manipulator is then able to live rent-free in your head! This is extremely dangerous behavior because it allows for self-doubt to be reinforced and allows for the manipulator to instill dangerous thoughts and ideas into someone's head.

The main thing to look out for in someone who behaves like this is how they were in past relationships if you see a pattern of them avoiding any responsibility for their actions then run away immediately. Manipulators can accomplish gaslighting through a variety of ways the main method in which they try to manipulate you is by breaking you down over time, slowly wearing away at you with the same line of garbage over and over again till you are forced to believe it. Once a narcissist has convinced you of their positioning it is very difficult to get a clear view, they obfuscate the truth and lie at every chance they have to try and get you on their side. They'll make you feel guilty for not going along with their behavior

The fact that this happens over a slow time is what makes it so damaging, it becomes difficult for you to realize that the behavior you are being presented with isn't normal, and usually by the time you have realized it is already too late. Narcissists are great at luring you back into their grips through very clever manipulation tricks, by subtly getting you to doubt yourself they slowly hook their tendrils into every aspect of your life until you feel powerless without them. The trick to getting past this kind of manipulation is just biting the bullet and running away. This can be hard to do because narcissists are very charming and good at convincing you, they will change. But the truth is a narcissist is never going to change their manipulative behavior is only going to get worse and continue. One of the narcissist's other dangerous weapons is to break down self-esteem in others. For instance, imagine you're an architecture and you are working on a new model for a house. Your manager gives you the rough blueprint, which you noticed there are a few areas that could use some improvements. You begin sketching your blueprint version and proceed to make a cardboard model of what they envisioned. A week later, your manager comes to see your progress, to which her face shows frustration. Raising her voice, she points out the different designs from hers, comments on how the rooms look too small and talk about how the deadline is in two weeks. Situations like these, where you are bombarded with criticism, figure out if what they're saying is constructive or destructive. Whichever one you decide it is, you want the person to get all their criticism out before trying to amend what you have done, since they will most likely ignore you while in such a state. Quietly take their words and wait until they're finished.

Afterward, explain whatever changes you made and your reasons for doing such a thing.

It is always good to know before being confronted if the change was worth it or not, so make sure to evaluate all your decisions. In any case, ask her to clarify her opinion. There is a good chance she will explain what she meant. However, if she were to dismiss your explanations and continue criticizing, at that point you can safely take her words for a grain of salt. And realize that the comments may not be reflective of what is truly going on in the situation. And instead, consider that what she is saying may simply be an attempt to manipulate you and get you to do something she wants.

Accepting that you are in a destructive relationship with a narcissist. Can be a difficult thing to do but once you start to look at all the signs together it ends up making sense. Someone who is going out of their way and lies and get you to believe things only through their worldview is not someone you want to be with. That is perhaps the saddest part of the manipulation. It doesn't tend to change and happens to only get worse as time moves on. Taking this examination of a relationship to the heart is required evil in the world we live in today. Perhaps arguably the most common form of manipulation in today's fast-paced society is the manipulation that salespeople will try and use on us.

Most sales tactics play on simple human emotions such as need or desire, and very specific fears like a fear of missing out or not belonging. Advertisements target us so subtly that we do not realize we are being taken for a ride until we make a purchase that we do not need. By using fancy colors and enticing cinematic, advertisements can play on very primal parts of our brain and get us to do what they want.

Look at the newest advertisements for the iPhone, and how they show people who happy while using their fancy brand-new iPhone. Are they truly happy because of their new iPhone or is it perhaps the situations they are shown in?

The first step any successful advertisement has to take in getting you to buy its product is to convince you that you need it. How can they sell you something if you don't need it?   Simple, they do so by creating these huge social media marketing campaigns in which they show thousands of people lining up to buy the newest and greatest fancy phone. They can convince you that if you want to be one of the cool kids that you should also buy into needing something you don't need at all, such as the new iPhone.

This manipulation works by playing on a psychological concept called "the fear of missing out". Your fear of not keeping up with the curve will entice you to buy the product even if it sets you back financially and even if you don't need it. You may have noticed how in lots of stores the kid's toys are all colorfully lit and have cool and interesting cut-outs designed to catch the attention of your little tyke. These bright colors and exciting stimuli fire up the reward centers of our brains and get us primed to make a purchase.

CHAPTER 9

RECLAIMING YOUR IDENTITY

RECOMMENDED ACTIVITIES

If you have been in a relationship with a narcissist, you have lost some sense of your own identity because that narcissist tried to make you part of their identity. Narcissists have issues with boundaries, so they saw you as an extension of themselves. Being treated as if you were an extension of someone else is bound to have made you feel less like yourself. You should not have to feel that way anymore. You should be able to feel like yourself again.

Interviewing Yourself

Sometimes it is hard to ask the right questions. Sometimes an open-ended question like, "How was your day?" is too quickly answered with a single word like, "Fine." The art of the interview is to ask the kinds of questions that require fleshed out responses that bring about new questions. Interview yourself and get them comfortable asking yourself what you think about the matter at hand. An interview requires self-reflection and a sense of identity.

One activity involved in the interviewing process is coming up with the right questions to ask. Think about what kinds of questions you wish someone would ask you. Think about the kinds of questions you ask other people naturally.

Guide yourself through the process of formulating questions as if you were guiding someone else preparing an interview for you. Acknowledge the difference between open-ended questions and closed questions. Then, make a list of open-ended questions to which only you have the answers.

A second activity that follows right along from the previous one is coming up with a list of questions to ask someone else. To make this a team effort, ask someone else what kinds of questions they would like for you to ask them. Or, ask them what kinds of questions they would like to be asked if they were interviewed.

Think about the differences between the kinds of questions they wish to be asked and the kinds of questions you would like to be asked. Think about how these things make you different kinds of people and have to do with your different identities and personalities.

A third activity is asking other people the kinds of questions you asked yourself. Just like in the last activity, you can acknowledge the differences between their answers and your answers.

For a fourth activity, you might even go ahead and guess the answers you would expect to hear from them before you ask. See if they surprise you. Consider how much of your own thoughts, desires, and personality traits went into your guesswork.

Consider how faulty your guesswork might be if you aren't actually answering questions because you assume you know the answers. Acknowledge the differences between your guesses and the answers.

A fifth activity is to actually discuss your guesswork with the other person. Discuss the benefits of anticipating answers. Discuss the possible negative effects of anticipating answers. Discuss when it is best to ask even if one thinks one knows the answer.

A sixth activity is writing or typing out your answer to a question you found particularly interesting. This could be the answer someone else gave you to a question that you thought was strange because it was so different from yours. This could be an answer you came up with that surprised even you. The point is just to sit down and give a little more thought to this activity by writing or typing it out.

A seventh activity is actually recording yourself as if you were responding to an interview question and then watching that recording. See how you express yourself. See if the person in the recording looks different than the person you generally believe yourself to be.

If you think it might be helpful, ask yourself how the narcissist you were with saw you. Consider the difference between all of these different notions of yourself. Finally, think about who you want to be.

An eighth activity is finding someone else to interview over Snapchat or some social media app like that. It is pretty easy to send someone a video asking them an open-ended question. Play around with this and observe how the two of you express yourself when being questioned and having a little time to watch yourself send each other recorded responses. Get to know yourself the way someone who communicates with you through such means would know you.

A ninth activity is revisiting the previous discussion about anticipating answers. Once you have spent a little more time playing around with these interview-style conversations, think about how much you learned that you could never have guessed. Apply this to yourself now. Do you ever make assumptions about yourself that turn out not to be true? Surely you have guessed that you would not like something that you turned out to like more than expected.

A tenth activity is to reflect on the difference between casual conversation and an interview. Consider what you have learned about your identity. Consider how to keep this practice going in a way that is healthy and helpful to you. It does not have to be as formal as the descriptions above.

The point is to start asking yourself and other meaningful questions that you can learn from but you must be active about getting started. Casual conversation has a way of being the default most of the time.

Reinvigorating Your Sense Perceptions

Considering the power of one's own power of senses promotes self-awareness.

One well-known activity that concerns the sense of sight is the game I-Spy. You should play I-Spy with yourself to awaken your interactive sense of sight. Select one thing that you see and study that thing with your eyes. See how your eyes focus. See how difficult it is for you to focus on one thing. See how long you can focus on that one thing. See if you learn anything from focusing on that one thing.

A second activity is to make an I-Hear version of I-Spy. Follow the same instructions. Be quiet. Try to tune into one thing. Listen to it as well as you can. Listen to it as long as you can. Listen to something else if something else becomes too loud to hear the last thing you tried to listen to. Just try to close your eyes and listen to something, anything.

A third activity is to make an I-Touch version of I-Spy. Touch something that feels good. Think about why it feels good. Think about the appropriate ways to touch that thing that feels good. Think about gentleness and what it means. Think about your ability to be gentle. Feel good about yourself for being able to touch something gently.

A fourth activity is to turn I-Spy into I-Smell. This one will be particularly fun in the kitchen or the backyard. Same rules apply. Choose one smell. Think about how you would explain a single smell to someone who had never smelled that thing before. You might notice that smells are nearly impossible to describe without simply comparing to other smells.

A fifth activity is to turn I-Spy into I-Taste. This might be fun to do with some kind of baked good or anything with complicated ingredients. Try to guess what each ingredient is. See how advanced your palate is.

A sixth activity is to play I-Spy with yourself in the mirror. Look at yourself. What do you see? Find one thing to focus on. Focus on it until it means something new to you than it did before. Give some aspect of you the kind of attention you spent on the narcissist you were with. Determine that this part of you deserves this kind of attention.

A seventh activity is to play I-Hear with your own voice. Say something that you would like to hear yourself say. Focus on the way it sounds when you say it. If you don't like the way it sounds at first, say it until you do like the way it sounds. Once you've figured out how to say it the way you want it to sound, repeat it like that several times.

An eighth activity is to play I-Smell with your own hair, room, or otherwise personal kind of aroma. Find a smell that you find particularly pleasant that has to do with you. It should be a smell that you identify with or someone has identified with you. Smell it as such. Think about how this smell is related to you, your space, and your identity.

A ninth activity is to play I-touch with your own body or personal space. Find something to touch that is either on your person or in your personal space. Touch it gently. Think about how it feels. Once again, be sure that you are giving the kind of attention you used to give to the narcissist to whatever it is you are touching. Remember the ways in which whatever you are touching is tied to your identity. Think about what this means to you.

A tenth activity is to play I-taste with your own cooking and knowing the ingredients you used. Cook something you love to eat. Think about every ingredient. When you taste it, try to recall each ingredient. See if you can taste each ingredient. Give yourself credit for your work. Appreciate the work you've done in the way you always hoped to receive appreciation from the narcissist you were in a relationship with.

Therapy

It's really important that you go to therapy for help reclaiming your identity. Therapy is one place that is guaranteed to be all about your project of learning how to be yourself and live productively with yourself and others.

Identifying your personal struggles will be welcomed and safely guided by someone familiar with narcissistic abuse. Your therapist will give you options that are tailored to your personal needs based on the type of abuse you experienced.

Counseling sessions are good for providing relief and emotional catharsis as well as proper guidance toward healing and recovery. If your goal is to reclaim your identity, you should tell your therapist about your intention. Therapy will be a place where you can safely share your experience of narcissistic abuse while making your way toward recovery. You will receive affirmation that what you experienced was in fact abuse from a person with narcissistic personality disorder. Your therapist may even be open to helping you better understand the narcissist you were in a relationship if you and your therapist decide it would be helpful for you.

Therapy is all about reclaiming one's identity because everything about it is geared toward the betterment of the patient. Therapy is one place where you know it will be all about you, which is a big step from where you were when you were with a narcissist.

When you were with a narcissist, it was all about them. The best way for you to start recovering and reclaiming your identity is to find a place where it can be all about you for an hour or so. You may not be comfortable making it all about you at first but you will find that it is helpful to do so. It is quite possible that you have lost a lot of yourself. Finding yourself may require a little help from a professional.

That said, the activities in this book should continue to help you with or without therapy. You will be better off with these activities than without making any moves toward your recovery.

You will be best off using these activities to supplement the work you are doing in therapy. Make sure you find the right therapist. Therapists are usually more than willing to help you find the right person even if it turns out they are not the right person for you.

Don't be afraid to tell the first therapist you try that you might be looking for something else. They'll be glad to help you find what you're looking for. Remember that there are a lot of different kinds of therapy and counseling for you to seek and settle into.

CHAPTER 10

SOME PERSONALITIES STRUGGLE MORE

I have noticed something interesting that may help people understand how or why they are targeted and to adjust accordingly. I have seen people being targeted by evil according to their personalities. This does not take into account any psychological disorders or mental illness that a person may have, but rather a discussion about a few quirks we may see in each other that we are either born with or that have been deeply planted into us. I try to understand how these factors play into the complexity of issues we may struggle with. Obviously, I will not cover every single personality quirk here. That is most likely impossible. This is only an exercise in noticing differences and how they play into the big picture.

The Bittersweet Personality

One personality that I have witnessed that has special issues with life situations is what I call "bittersweet". This is not anyone's fault. We are given these traits by God when we are born, as many mothers know by watching more than one of their small children even from an infant. The BitterSweet personality often has a very strong sense of justice, so it will be harder for this person to simply shrug off injustices, forgive, let go, and trust that God will take care of it in time. They are acutely aware of things being unequal or out of balance, even down to physical things in the physical world around them being off center.

Perhaps these people are better suited for situations in life and jobs where high levels of discretion and judgment are required. The BitterSweet personality tends to highly appreciate the sweetness of life, but is also deeply wounded by bitter things. You cannot simply tell these people to grow a thicker skin and toughen up. They will see right through that as a lack of intelligence on your part for not understanding reality very deeply. If you have this sensitivity, it is just one more reason to strengthen your faith. If you have these tendencies, you will need every bit of grace and protection God has to offer.

Oversized Conscience

This one is actually mostly good to have. You want an oversized conscience more than an undersized one! When you have an oversized conscience, be super grateful that you are NOT a sociopath, like the growing number of them out there these days! Just pray for balance and understand that you will feel some things more acutely than most. If people are saying horrible lies about you, you may feel prone to guilt, even though you are innocent. One of the most evil attacks you will face as the sensitive, high-responsibility, or oversized conscience, is an attack of lies from a demonic sociopath. These types of people understand that if they can catch you in a no-win, double bind, or crazy-making situation, that you will suffer from false guilt, shame, or confusion for possibly the rest of your life.

You may feel the acuteness of the evil of harm caused by other people more strongly than other people can understand. This type of person may live a larger part of their life ASSUMING what God's future wills and plans for their life is, and rush God's timing or be off completely. Instead of focusing on the daily importance of growing deep in God's love, they may get caught up more easily with fears that they are missing "God's Will" for their life because they did not go to a specific school or take a particular occupation. Sometimes God is leading us to take a very specific step in life, but these people are not balanced in this area and may have a hard time with it, beating themselves up and constantly thinking they have missed God's plan or timing.

They may also struggle with receiving grace and rely upon their own works more than they should, due to their emotional attachment to guilt. They may be more susceptible to attacks of false guilt. Just don't use this as an excuse. A good conscience is necessary, and you don't want a seared one! Don't let it stop you from relying upon the Lord, not your own works, and don't let it keep you in constant tormenting guilt, shame, or fear that may be holding you back from truly walking with fullness in God.

Another note on excessive guilt, these types can be "people pleasers" and feel they never do enough. They may find themselves a victim of users more often. If the user person abuses a big conscience person, the big conscience very often feels guilty as though they should have done more, when this is the very opposite of true. When the big conscience needs to take a stand against evil, they will often beat themselves up about how they took this stand, especially if they were passionate in the way they did it. It is always good to question these things, but not to live in any torment when you do your best.

If you find yourself a victim of this situation where an abuser wronged you, and you are taking a lot of false blame or guilt, you can try to get in a quiet place and pray to God to help you see clearly. You may use Bible verses of truth against the abuser's lies, and journal, pray, and talk to close people about your struggle. Have two or three Christian friends agree on earth against the lies against you. There is power in two or three Christians agreeing as witnesses together against the lies. Bind in heaven and on earth the lies and blame that are coming against you falsely. People have also reported successfully telling their brains or part of themselves to calm down unnecessary excessive guilt. In some cases, you may need psychological help if you are receiving such a violent attack to your sensitive mind and spirit by cruel people.

Hypersensitive Personality

A person can be hypersensitive in many ways. It may be physically to cold, emotionally to music, allergic to foods and medication, or sensory processes such as saliva and sweating may seem to work overtime as compared to others. If the problem is overactive nerves, there may be racing thoughts or panic attacks.

You may be in situations where the hunger or cold make you so uncomfortable that you feel like screaming, but others around you look bored or half asleep as though unaware of pain. If you bring up these painful scenarios later, the other people that were in that same situation look at you funny and wonder what you are talking about.

The gift of overactive nerves is that you process information very quickly, learn fast, and tend to score high on tests. When a hypersensitive person is harmed, they will feel the pain more than others and for much longer. This is not a lack of forgiveness, but a tendency to feel more acutely. Knowing this helps you to accept it and deal with it, rather than blaming yourself for hurting more than necessary on purpose. Each of us is born with different abilities and gifts, and when you draw close to the Lord, you may be surprised at how what you once thought was a weakness is used for God in some unexpected way.

The Wounded Spirit

This is not really a personality trait, as much as a very serious condition that will shape you for life and make you vulnerable in certain ways. The scripture says, The wounded spirit who can bear? (Proverbs 18:14) The best thing to know about a wounded spirit is that you can only really get healing through God over time, and do not blame yourself if you need extra care. In these last days, many people will endure wounded, crippled and broken spirits, and the Lord may allow you to endure a long season of this to prepare you for the deeper and eternal things of God or as a witness against evil on the earth. It is a special position to be entrusted with being such a witness against evil on this earth, and even a greater testimony as we overcome this evil and stand in agreement with God against it. Many people will become wounded soldiers in the wars of the end time evil - physically, mentally, and spiritually. Beware of unhealthy distractions, addictions, and traps that you may be vulnerable to because of the pain in your life, and draw closer to God than ever before.

The Caretaker

The Caretaker tends to be similar to the Oversized Conscience in which they do not feel right, or do not feel they have fulfilled a proper obligation unless they are rescuing everyone or constantly solving people's problems. When this is seen in the extreme, it may be a control or a self esteem issue. Overall, it is better to err on the side of being overly giving toward others than to be callous and abusive. The Caretaker and Oversized Conscience are more likely to be rewarded in this life and the next for their genuine actions, but they would sometimes be better off with more of a balanced understanding.

The Caretaker can make good firemen, police, counselors, or nurses. They are less likely to recognize balance and the need for self-care, and easily take on too much responsibility. They may have a problem saying 'No' or they may get used a lot. They may constantly stress their spouse, who sees them as too weak and inconsiderate to say no for the benefit of the family. They may be rewarded for any service they meant unto the Lord for his work, but they are prone to burnout if they cannot see that their sense of duty is out of balance. Another problem they may have is enabling addicts or abusers with their overprotective and bleeding-heart ways.

I am sure you can think of other personality quirks than the ones I have listed here, that make life more difficult or easier in some ways. You may find it interesting to read about business analysts who study people for success in personnel, hiring, or sales and who have identified common personality categories such as Too Honest, Perfectionist, Big Thinker, and Overly Committed. Being aware of genuine differences can help you forbear other people who are going through things or have strange reactions. It is good to be aware of your own vulnerabilities because your enemy is aware, and he will take advantage! Being aware can help you understand, bear through, pray specifically, and perhaps develop unique defenses for your specific situation.

CHAPTER 11

EMPATH & NARCISSIST

A VERY DANGEROUS ATTRACTION

There is no relationship as painful and dangerous than that with a narcissist. The categorizing of these relationships are carried by making use of several kinds of abuse, which are: exploitation, gas-lighting, manipulation, disregard, and physical/verbal/mental/emotional/financial abuse. Empaths are seen to be generous, kind, deeply plugged into people's emotions, and have more information about people than they do about their selves. Encountering a narcissist is an unlucky situation that doesn't involve only empaths. The empaths are mostly entangled with a pathological narcissist when compared to other people, this needs more investigations as it seems unlikely paring in so many ways.

NOTE: "He" and "she" are used for narcissists and empaths respectively, and was done to making reading easy, and you should not assume that the personalities are gender inclined. The abilities of the narcissists and empaths are not gender-dependent.

Who is an Empath?

People who are specially and exquisitely tuned into other people's emotions are known as Empaths, to a point where these emotions are felt. The Empaths are kind, nurturing, and sensitive helplessly, and they tend to put other people's needs before theirs. This is the major reason why they attract narcissists.

Who is a Narcissist?

They are self-centered, morally, and emotionally deficient people who have to the tendency of having an empathic feeling for others. Other person's feelings are not taken into consideration by them because they have no idea that they have feelings as much as they do.

These two sets of people being remotely attracted to each other make no sense, not to talk of them forming bonds that are unbreakable and nearly fatal, but it usually happens. But how?

The reason why a narcissist is attracted to an empath can be seen at first glance. Everything the narcissist lacks, e.g. care, emotions, kindness, support, self-control, making friends, and transparency, are all features of an empath, the narcissist, therefore, strives to covet these things from whoever possesses them or ruin them to ensure that no one has it. The empath portrays herself as a glowing beacon and freely gives herself to the narcissist, this is in the form of waving a red flag for a bull. Just like a never-dying battery, he senses indefinitely a source which he can leech off. He can continuously take from the empath and in return she continuously gives, this is an unchangeable nature of the empath-narcissist relationship.

Why is the empathy so attracted to the narcissist? The narcissist's powerful vibe at the onset will resonate within the empathy deeply. The narcissist captures her attention, and she is magnetically attracted to him as he is to her. The presence of the narcissist is emotionally intense and that attracts most empaths, whether the empath realizes it or not. Reading his emotions are difficult, though he gives off an intense vibe but it is distorted e.g. something static on a TV where the true image cannot be seen, and for the fact that empaths find it easy to read other people's emotions, she will be drawn to him in other to figure him out. Who is he? What is his current condition? What is he all about? Together with his well-drafted pitch showing his wonderful nature and her wonderful nature as well, he will also unveil his lifetime of abuse, he will successfully snare her because she does not know that his emotionally intense nature has nothing to do with her.

It shouldn't be possible for the empath to fall for it because she easily reads people' emotions and understands their true selves. She possibly can she what he truly is, as most empaths tense to perceive that something is wrong him often during their first conversation, she also tends to perceive something else which overrides the initial suspicious feeling, and this includes; how broken the narcissist is asides all his lies and abuse. The narcissist brokenness is not an act by him nor a mistake by her but that he is broken. So many narcissists are very good a looking lost and helpless because they are in several ways. She didn't make a mistake in reading him but in assuming he can be helped.

The attraction is there because she wants to help him, and this is her blind spot because he cannot be helped or pieced together, and besides does not want to. Even when she has gotten a better view of this, his wounds become clearer to her, and this is obvious in everything he is doing especially the horrible ones

The Why

The narcissist is highly-skilled at ensuring that she feels that she is the only one who can help him, or that she has helped him already and this is precisely what she desires. The empath has a desire to help him, and he is unbelievably convincing which the fact that he constantly praises and emotionally entices her to get a response. She ends up supplying him with the emotional sustenance he desires, and this ensures that she continuously showers care and attention on him. This is a disastrous co-dependence which focuses on satisfying one party who can never be satisfied. He is like a hollow cup which never gets filled up no matter how much you pour into it.

The empath in this relationship also needs to be fulfilled even those this does not ever seem to be the case. The empath is always the injured party, but she gets injured willingly, she has ended up caged in a relationship with someone who will always need her help. The empath has factually conjured up a career out of caring for a victim who does not desire to get better. To some people, this may look like victim-blame, but the empath can only get away from the narcissist for good by realizing that it is her choice if she stays and she can always choose to leave and that they only power he has over her is the one she gave to him.

Many narcissists are seen to be arrogant overachievers but tend to be a cripple in several ways by their disorder of not properly function in the environment not just superficially. The opportunity of taking care of someone in perpetuity is perceived by the empath, and even if she has no intentions of helping him, he nature can make her feel it is her obligation. How will he cope in her absence? Despite his horrible nature, abandoning him doesn't seem fair due to his sickness is not his fault. The workability of his brain is not his fault, perhaps he wasn't loved enough when he was an infant, or he was abused, none of it might be his fault. Anyways, this is also definitely not the fault of the empath either, and do not deserve the punishment for someone else's mistake. She will be forever punished if she decides to remain in the relationship. Refusal to help people in need of her help is the empaths nightmare, especially when she could have helped them. Though she cannot help it, her logic is faulty.

CHAPTER 12

GETTING RID OF NEGATIVE INTROJECTION

The process of trying to save the relationship with your narcissistic father is long and arduous. It is not easy to understand why he put you through years of emotional abuse. What makes it even more difficult is that while you're trying to find answers to your questions, you are also trying to patch yourself up and learning to appreciate yourself for who you truly are and accept your lot in life.

Many victims of narcissistic behavior react by moving towards closure as fast as they possibly can. It is their choice because they do not have a clear understanding of what narcissistic personality disorder is. Closure will not make the negative things magically go away, but it can make you feel dead inside. What you need is to find a middle ground wherein you can learn to discriminate every negative opinion or comment hurled at you.

You have to keep in mind that you do not have to absorb all the harsh and hateful comments about you. What you need is to learn to evaluate all the negative things before you accept them as true. If you know that they are not valid, you can disregard them like rubbish. Of course, this is easier said than down because you've been raised and exposed to extremes. There was never a middle ground and it's a huge challenge to find it.

Even if you've reconnected with your slightly mellowed down version of your father, there will always be that restrictive narcissistic father residing in your head, feeding you negative words. It's like the voice of criticism that makes you feel deficient. It stops you from trusting yourself and it prevents you from taking the necessary steps to change your outlook in life.

The problem with having unwanted negative criticisms in your head is that no matter how much you hate them, you succumb to the messages and believe them to be true. You want to reject the false inputs, but you have no clue how and where to start. Your response to the negative thoughts is key to learning how to reject them.

Silencing Negative Introjection

Introjection occurs when you internalize the ideas of other people. In the context of your relationship with your father, it is his negative ideas that reside in your mind. You adopt his beliefs about you even if they are far from the truth. You identify with his distorted ideologies reflexively without evaluation or analysis.

Sigmund Freud characterized introjection as a defense mechanism usually used by children or adults to cope with parents who are emotionally unavailable. That judgmental voice in your head continues to reassure you that a little bit of your father is present even if he is not. If the negative introjection lingers, you will never get rid of feelings of worthlessness, incompetence, and deficiency. You'll find it difficult to find your true sense of self.

If left unchecked, the negative introjection will make you become self-critical. Internal conflict may also arise because you are unable to reconcile inconsistent concepts—your longing for your father's attention and the ill-effects of his narcissism on you.

You need to understand that the measure of emotional and mental health is the state of self. If you are experiencing an overwhelming inner turmoil, then it means you are far from being in a healthy state. Silencing the negative introjection requires deliberate and purposeful thought and effort. You need to treat it as foreign to your own self. It is not supposed to be there, and it is overstaying its welcome. You need to isolate it by identifying it as a non-self. It involves changing loyalties.

When you were raised by a narcissistic father and perhaps an enabling mother, your loyalty to your father outweighs your loyalty to yourself. If you try to reverse the situation and put yourself first, you will be adjudged as selfish. This is where the inner conflict comes in. You want the circumstances to change but the conflict within you prevents you from taking your side.

Perhaps the silver lining is that negative introjection is not always at full strength. There are times when it is strong and at times, it is so weak that you can ignore it completely. It is a long-term battle with your own self, but outside intervention can make lasting changes. Therapy helps to bring back logic which weakens the introjection.

Setting yourself free from the negative introjection requires removing the childhood expectations developed early in life. The pressure that it brings makes you think that your child self is in charge of your being. But you have to understand that you are now an adult with adult needs, expectations and responsibilities. Your childish desire for your narcissistic father to meet your needs and expectations is just wishful thinking. Your adult self should remove the addicting illusory expectations from your system by getting inputs from people who are fighting a similar battle.

Group therapy can truly help you see that you are not alone in your ordeal. There are other people like you who have a negative self-image because they were raised by a narcissistic parent.

Your distorted image of your self can be cut by relating to someone who can provide you love and affection. When you are loved and nurtured, the negative introjection will loosen its grip on you.

Children of narcissistic fathers are often taught that there is only perfection and failure; there is nothing in between. This is a limited view of life because there is no more room for improvement and growth. If you can open yourself to creativity, you'll see that there are a whole spectrum of visions and infinite dreams. You'll realize that life is not just perfection or failure; there's so much in between that makes life worth living. Creativity allows you to become the person that you've always wanted to be. You'll remember the pleasures you get when you have the freedom to do things your way.

You do not have to always meet an external standard set by your father. You are so much more than your father's opinion about yourself. The problem is that the years of being under the watchful eye of your father taught you to overvalue what you receive from him and undervalue what you are capable of. You've probably lost the ability to think clearly for yourself because your ideas are always criticized and adjudged as wrong and invalid. Every reaction you get from him is a form of condemnation. The result is that you become afraid to satisfy your own personal desires. You always measure yourself based on the unrealistic metrics set out for you, knowing full well that you would never meet them.

When you learn to separate yourself from those standards, you will realize that your values and happiness need not be tied to your father's measure of success such as money, fame, beauty, and power. There's more to life than trying to impress your narcissistic father whose values are flawed and distorted to serve his sense of grandeur.

It is unfortunate that your life and vision are shaped by a narcissistic father who wanted you to see the world his way. His aggressive and destructive pride harms you in ways that he would never acknowledge. He doesn't realize that while he was busy fulfilling his wishes and desires, he is hurting you deeply. Although he makes you feel that you are an extension of himself, you end up having a completely different experience from him. His needs are satisfied, while your own needs are barely heeded. You always get the short of the stick. If you so much try to break his protective reverie by standing your ground, you get the brunt of a horrible reaction. He is too blinded by his self-centeredness that he fails to see your motives and desires. The critical reactions that you get from him cause additional pain.

The narcissistic falsehoods that were fed to you can cause nothing but misery because you are trained to act in ways that please only one person. It was always about him and never really about you. When you don't measure up, you expose your weakness, which only makes him stronger albeit superficially hence it strengthens the ego.

You didn't have a choice as a child but you do now

WHY YOU FEEL GUILTY AND WHY YOU SHOULD NOT. IT IS NOT YOUR FAULT

What if you weren't right all the while about your mother being a narcissist? What happens if you are the one we should be asking her to run away from? What if she is not a narcissist and you are? Is it possible?

This shouldn't matter and never will. What matters the most is how you feel. They are yours, so treat them like you would what you love. How long you have been with your mother whether it has been a while or not or whether you are still with her or you've left her long ago doesn't matter more than your emotions; how you feel now. You wouldn't be reading this book if you weren't attracted to it based on how you think and the confusing questions that have stubbornly refused to leave your head: How could your mother be hard on you despite the fact you love her? Who do I love, and can I really find them? You wouldn't require answers for these questions if you didn't develop a fake self that was created in you by your mother. This necessarily didn't get into your head with building materials and a construction company to set this edifice, but they created the enabling environment that left you with no choice other than to create a self you would believe in and express your feelings towards. Suddenly, you have noticed all that glittered about yourself and mother was never gold, you always believed she thought the best for you and instead you were the one who refused to comply. The problem with the abuse is that it is psychological, making it hard to deal with. To the Narcissist, you are worthless, and I can imagine how many times you broke down because of how your mother treated you. The treatment will never improve positively in case you want to stay around and hope it gets better, but be sure she will keep using the implements she used to lure you into loving and admiring her no matter what she does.

Your mother always made you believe what she wanted you to believe. I don't need to ask if she did because that's her greatest weapon. Look back, and you'll understand what I mean. She will continue doing the same thing over and over again if you don't decide to bring an end to the bouts of abuse you have endured. You can't allow what she's trying to make you believe sink in anymore. You want an honest answer from the narcissist regarding where you got it wrong, but this will never come by. Instead, you are left blaming yourself because you can't seem to find the answer. You have already been made to believe you are the reason why you are abused and since that's the only thing you have internalized over the years, you just keep blaming yourself for what you didn't do.

It's not your fault, stop charging yourself with a crime you didn't commit. If you weren't living with your mother or another narcissist, you wouldn't be feeling this way. After all, if she isn't a narcissist, she would have been honest and wouldn't have treated you this way from inception. So because you are with a mother who won't give you an honest answer and has blindfolded you with lies, you don't feel good anymore, and you have started doubting yourself. This isn't right and healthy for you. Are you a Narcissist? NO! A narcissist lacks empathy and will never understand how you feel because they believe they are superior and therefore have no need to pay attention to another's feelings. If you were a Narcissist, believe me, you won't be in this pit of doubt. You won't be critical of yourself, and there is no way you would be able to love someone. Narcissists don't blame themselves or doubt themselves.

It's still not wrong to feel the way you do about all these. No one can fault you for being the way you are or the way you feel. The feelings are yours, and I care about it that's why I am putting this out there so you can get it.

You are not responsible for how another person feels. How we feel is controlled by us, meaning all your mother blamed you for is a sign she has refused to make her feelings hers, so she sets out to keep you under her control. Now she's been able to do that; you notice you have doubted yourself and still do. It works on anyone like it is working on you. Now that you have seen the truth and known about the true color of your mother's nature, you now know it's not your fault.

As the award-winning American author Dr. Elan Golomb described in her novel; Trapped in the Mirror, a book which showed the experiences and aftermaths of children who had narcissist parents and grew up to become adults with different wrong attitudes shaped by their defected parenting, children with a narcissistic parent may end up like their parents. A lot of them ended up showing attributes of anger, self-loathing in the form of anorexia, bulimia, etc. poor performances at work, with problems in their relationships. It is therefore not strange to see some of the traits your parents attributed being manifested in your own life.

Let us now focus on the topic; why you feel guilty. This is simply because some of the traits you dislike in your narcissistic mother has begun to manifest in your own life, and you can't seem to understand why. You thought it was impossible as you swore on several occasions not to be like her. Now, you have begun to detest yourself and everyone around you. You ask questions no one seems to want to answer, and many people avoid coming to you because of your outburst of anger and arrogance. Others are becoming afraid of your personality, and they are frightened to open up to you, at least to give you an insight into who you are becoming. For those who are close enough to confront you, who feel an obligation to tell you when you are going wrong, they find it difficult to show you the damage you are causing because you have refused to see anything from the perspective of others. Your life has now become an island, one deserted by all, due to its unproductivity and effects on others. This is a major reason you feel guilty. You feel guilty because you have lost control (you thought you had control of everything whereas, you were never in control of anything). And all you seem to have achieved is plummeting downwards before your very eyes.

Why should you not feel guilty? Very simple. It was never your fault. You didn't choose the family to come from. You were not there at the time of the formative years of your narcissistic mother. You could not have changed anything. And usually, your parents are your first role models. You started learning the basics of life from them. They formed the principles that guided your survival instinct. And it's not strange for most children to gravitate towards their mother because of the motherly affection they get. Their mothers are mostly around when they need help. So, it should not be a surprise that you have a similar attitude to that of your narcissistic mother. This is because having a mother with a narcissistic personality disorder most likely would be a major player in your character trait having a big role in shaping who you eventually become.

Don't believe the lie the narcissist tells you that you are always at fault. Their hobby is to slander people, gaslight them, and keep hovering like a hawk over the times you hurt them or refused to submit or something. Don't give in to this; it's part of the script they are acting. Day to day they act it out. Don't be caught up in this deceit; they are careful about their actions. Even if she wasn't diagnosed with the disorder and she perfectly fits the criteria we have listed out, you are free to tag her that. It's your choice; you are not in the wrong.

In the long run, what is right or wrong won't matter anymore. What matters the most is that you are on to live the life you so desired; a happy one. You realize this now it's better. It isn't late as long as you are ready to move on to aid your recovery. Your recovery sure wouldn't come in a night, but it will. Time heals. Don't let yourself drown in the ocean of doubt again, don't hate yourself, love who you are going to become and your feelings. BELIEVE IN YOURSELF.

CHAPTER 13

TIPS TO DISARM NARCISSISTS

You have spent far too long as a victim. Know that as you escape the narcissist, you shift from a victim to a survivor—you have survived. It is time to remove that victim mentality, in which you feel as though you are powerless and worthless and create a sense of worth for yourself. You can achieve freedom through your actions and behaviors, and you can allow yourself to escape the title of victim. Through caring for yourself and following these steps, you are able to remove the victimized part of yourself and focus on healing. You can do this if you put your mind to it. No one has to remain a victim of circumstances or abuse forever, and you can prove that you are a fighter and a survivor in reclaiming your freedom. You belong to no one. You can set yourself free.

Acknowledge the Abuse

The first step in healing from abuse is acknowledgment. You need to acknowledge that there is a problem. That problem, in this instance, is the narcissistic abuse you have endured. If you want to heal, you must be able to look at what happened and accurately identify it for what it was—abuse. Those who cannot open their eyes to this truth really struggle to heal as they deny what they have been through. They deny that what they have gone through is traumatic, and they deny that the fault of the abuse lies solely with the abuser.

Oftentimes, before the acknowledgment stage is achieved, the victim frequently finds herself defending the narcissist. She cannot begin to heal from his abuse and free herself if all she does is make excuses for his actions and abuse. Instead, she will be too preoccupied attempting to validate it somehow, which directly invalidates her own suffering. She fails to see that she has been suffering through abuse, whether due to denial or truly not seeing the abuse for what it is, and she cannot really free herself from abuse that she refuses to acknowledge is right there.

Remember, just because you have acknowledged the abuse does not mean that you are weak, worthless, or deserve judgment to be passed on you. It simply means that you were abused by a bad person who chose to take advantage of the situation. This does not reflect poorly on you, and you are not to blame.

Discovering Support Groups and Networks

As you heal, it can be incredibly useful to discover support groups. They are there to aid you in your healing process, as well as to provide you with people you can talk to that understand what you have gone through. You are able to discover several different people that will be able to understand what your abuse entailed, as well as being able to provide you advice from the perspective of having been there before. While it is easy for people who have never been through narcissistic abuse to offer their perspectives and reading a book such as this one can have invaluable information within it, it really does sometimes help to be able to speak to someone one-on-one.

When you join a support group for narcissistic abuse victims, you will be able to understand better what the healing process entails. You will be able to speak to people who are at various points in their own healing. You will be able to hear other people's stories and understand more thoroughly what they have been through. You will be able to see that there is hope for your future in seeing other people at further points in their own lives and healing processes. When you see someone else who has healed from the abuse, you will see what your life can become, if you put in the effort to make it your life. You will see what lies ahead, and if you do hit a roadblock, you will be able to talk to other people who will understand. If you have a day of wanting to talk to someone about how much you miss the narcissist, these people, who understand that complicated feeling of loving their abusers, will understand. That kind of support can be absolutely invaluable when faced with the seemingly insurmountable healing process of getting over from the narcissist.

You can find support groups, both in-person and online on the internet. By searching for narcissistic abuse survivor support groups, you will find several sources, both in your local area and elsewhere. Even if there are not any groups local to you, you will at the very least be able to access groups online, and maybe even discover the resources to set up your own support group in person in your area. Narcissistic abuse is far too common, and it is highly unlikely that you are the only person within your immediate area that has suffered.

Therapy

Therapy is like vitamins—everyone can benefit from them. There are very few people that cannot truly benefit from therapy, and there are no reasons to be ashamed of seeking therapy if you think that is what you will need to get over the narcissist and move on with your life. A therapist can help you work through your problems, guiding you through healthier problem-solving techniques that could benefit you. They can offer you healthy coping mechanisms and teach you how to utilize them. They can also lend a quiet ear to listen as you discuss your own feelings, thoughts, and opinions.

Therapy can also provide some valuable insight into why you became a target of abuse in the first place. The therapist will be able to identify some of the personality traits that have rendered you vulnerable to narcissistic abuse, and can also help you cover up those weaknesses, so they cannot be exploited in the future. If you have cripplingly low self-esteem, for example, the therapist can help you work on strengthening your self-esteem and ensuring it does not get used against you again.

If you decide that a therapist would be a good choice for you, you have several options to aid you in discovering a therapist that you will click with. Remember, therapists, like doctors, are not one-size-fits-all people. There will be therapists with whom you will and will not click. There will be therapists that drive you insane, and there will be one that will seem like the perfect fit for you. Remember, discovering which therapist will work for you is absolutely a process, and you should not feel discouraged if the first one, two, or even three or four, do not quite mesh well with you. This does not mean that therapy will not be successful for you, only that you have not yet discovered a therapist that will work well for you.

There are several ways to locate therapists. You can start by asking your primary care doctor for a referral. The primary care physician can create a referral, which may be accepted by your insurance as a reason to pay for therapy. You can try searching online for therapists in your area and look for those who specialize in abuse or narcissistic abuse. You can also call your insurance provider and ask them for a list of therapists in your area that are in-network.

These days, you can even attend therapy over the internet, either with video or voice chat or through instant messengers and emails. These therapy types could be useful for people who struggle to speak to others in person, or who need a flexible schedule for their therapy that does not line up with standard business hours.

No matter the method you use for therapy, any of these are acceptable options. Each can provide you with information that will help you heal. Each can help you set yourself free from the spell of blame and guilt the narcissist has cast over you. Though you may be apprehensive at first, in time, you will likely come to find some value to speaking to a therapist.

Self-Care

Self-care is incredibly important, regardless of whether you have been abused or not. Everyone should engage in self-care regularly in order to feel better, happier, and more fulfilled. Narcissistic abuse victims, in particular, should also seek to engage in extra self-care after so long spent suffering under the thumb of the narcissist. Because the narcissist does not care about his victims, and taking time for self-care would have taken time away from the narcissist, he likely discouraged you from ever doing anything for yourself. If you tried to exercise, he may have insisted that you stop so he could have your attention, or even just because he wants you to be unhealthy to worsen your self-esteem. If you tried to spend time reading or doing your hobbies, he may have insisted that you stop because it took away from time that you should have spent catering to him.

When you are finally free, you may find that you are in desperate need of self-care. You deserve to spend some time tending to your own needs. Here are five different types of self-care that are essential to your mental health.

Physical self-care

Physical self-care involves anything that you are doing to feel better. You could spend a day watching your favorite movies or choose to work out and take care of yourself. Ultimately, what counts here is that you are doing something to your physical self in order to make your mental health better. Some of these will make you physically healthier while others are simply things you are doing that lower your stress while not improving general health. Here are a few examples of things you could do to engage in physical self-care:

- Cleaning up your diet and eating healthy, nourishing foods
- Exercising regularly and consistently to improve your physical health
- Spending the time to do your makeup if you enjoy wearing it
- Taking a relaxing bath
- Going on a calming walk

Emotional self-care

Emotional self-care is typically acknowledging your feelings and allowing them to happen without judging them. Remember, your feelings are fleeting and are simply feelings. They do not necessarily have to be acted upon, nor are they some sort of guide that has to dictate what you are doing. They also should not cause you to be ashamed or embarrassed. Acknowledging your feelings and allowing them to occur is for the best, as doing so enables you to recognize your feelings as legitimate and removes the shame you may feel. Some things you can do to engage in emotional self-care include:

- Crying when you feel the need to do so
- Spending time with those who make you laugh
- Stop and acknowledge whatever you are feeling in the moment
- Reflect and acknowledge the things that make you happy
- Practice mindfulness

Mental self-care

Mental self-care involves caring for your intellectual or mental self. This can involve making sure you keep yourself stimulated and engaged in your environment to avoid falling into the dredges of boredom. It also involves acknowledging thought processes and recognizing that we have different thoughts that can trigger different emotions. When you want to engage in mental self-care, you should take the time to pay attention to what you are feeling and why, as well as how you can change your current mental state to something calmer or happier. Some examples of mental self-care include:

- Reading a book
- Practice self-awareness
- Accepting your current situation or attempting to change it
- Focusing on the present rather than the past or future
- Finding something you are grateful for at that moment

Professional self-care

Oftentimes, your professional self gets left behind when attempting to engage in self-care. Remember that your professional life is a major part of who you are, and you should attempt to keep that professional self healthy as well. Ensure that you are happy in your job, that you enjoy your role, and that the tasks you are completing are not overwhelming or disheartening in any way. You want to ensure that your job is something pleasant, or at least tolerable for you. Here are some ways to work on your professional self:

- Work on your resume
- Brush up on some of your more important work-related skills
- Take a class to further your education
- Take a short break or vacation from work altogether

Social self-care

For the vast majority of people, life is incomplete without social relationships. Most people seek out some sort of social connections with other people, whether familial, romantic, or platonic, and that sort of self-care should always be encouraged. This sort of self-care will help you strengthen your relationships with those around you. Some examples of social self-care include:

- Date night with your friends
- Calling your parents regularly
- Joining groups that are about your interests and hobbies
- Texting your best friend

Hobbies and Healthy Outlets for Emotions

Remember that caring for yourself should also involve pursuing things that bring you pleasure. Set aside time in your life to spend working on your hobbies; even a small period of time in which you are able to work on your hobby can be incredibly satisfying and healing. Even if you have to say no to a friend or family member wanting to spend time with you, you should make it a point to make time for your hobby.

Along with hobbies, you should make it a point to engage in something that allows you to get the negative feelings out. Those who have spent extended periods of time with the narcissist oftentimes absorb a lot of the narcissist's negative emotions and those negative emotions have to be released somehow in order to heal. If left alone and ignored, the negativity will fester and build-up without relief, and that is the breeding ground of toxicity. You can release those negative emotions healthily through a wide range of ways. You could try working out to physically sweat out the negativity, creating art, writing, or doing anything else that helps you alleviate the stress.

Compassion for Yourself

When you are attempting to free yourself from victimhood, you should always make sure that you are compassionate with yourself. Through compassion, you will be able to forgive yourself if you feel as though you have slipped up. Maybe you attempted to contact the narcissist, or you did contact the narcissist. Though not ideal, this is okay. Be compassionate. People make mistakes, and people learn from their mistakes. Remind yourself that it is okay to make mistakes and move on. By remaining compassionate with yourself, you will make sure that you do not wrap your entire self-worth around whether you are successful or not. People everywhere fail, and you are not expected to be perfect.

Compassion and forgiving yourself is not the same as forgetting, however. You should always learn from your mistakes as you make them. This, at the very least, allows for you to find some sort of value in whatever mistake you happened to make. Finding the good in the bad will help you better cope with whatever has happened.

Grieving

When you are trying to heal yourself and free yourself of the narcissist's abuse, you oftentimes feel as though you are grieving. This is because you are. You are grieving the person you thought the narcissist was. You are grieving the loss of a relationship. You are grieving for the treatment you endured. This is normal and expected. Grief comes in five distinct stages, all of which you are likely to pass through as you heal.

Denial

Denial is the first stage of grief. At this point, you believe that the narcissist is not toxic or abusive, and you do whatever it takes to uphold that belief. You are happier not acknowledging the pain the narcissist has caused, preferring not to have to acknowledge the abuse for what it was. This stage may involve you telling yourself that the abuse was not so bad after all and that you can continue to tolerate it just fine.

Anger

The next stage of grief is anger. At this point, you have opened your eyes and acknowledge that yes, the narcissist was abusive. You are enraged by the fact that the narcissist has put you through so much abuse, and even the thought of him or what he has done is enough to send you into a rage.

Bargaining

At the bargaining stage, you begin to try to make deals with yourself, a god, or any other unseen power. You tell yourself that you will do anything to make the relationship go back to the way it was. You sort of blame yourself here, telling yourself that you will go back if the narcissist stops abusing and that you will stop doing whatever it is you think is triggering the narcissist to abuse you in the first place.

Depression

At this point, you recognize the gravity of the situation. You see that the narcissist will never change and that reality is exactly what you see in front of you. This thought is enough to trigger a state of depression as you realize that what you want is entirely unattainable. You want the narcissist to stop abusing you but to love you more than anything, but that is impossible, and the impossibility of it is devastating and difficult to manage.

Acceptance

The final stage of grief is acceptance. You have weathered the storm, muddling through the depression stage until you have finally begun to accept life for what it is. You understand the futility of trying to fight it off any longer and instead decide to accept reality. You know that you will never get what you want, and you are finally ready to live with that fact. Though it may be upsetting to you and even though you may still wish you could love the narcissist, you recognize that it will not happen, and you begin to feel as though you can live with that reality.

CHAPTER 14

ACKNOWLEDGING ABUSE

SETTING YOUR INTENTION TOWARD RECOVERY

Blaming the Victim and Other Stereotypes of Narcissistic Abuse

Victims of domestic violence are quite typically ashamed of what they have endured. No matter the kind of abuse endured, there are always stereotypes about what had happened and whether it was deserved or not, and many people prefer to remain quiet simply out of shame. They do not want to be shamed for going back to their abusers, or for being in an abusive relationship in the first place. Many of the reasons they are often shamed are also rooted in myth and stereotype. It is time to correct those negative stereotypes of abuse victims. After all, those who have suffered through the egregious abuse from the narcissist or other partners that chose to harm them, do not need to have their validity questioned or face the shame of being told that it was their fault.

Here are some of the most common myths and stereotypes about the victims of abuse.

If You Go Back to the Abuser, the Abuse Must Not Be That Bad(?)

Did you know it takes the average domestic violence victim seven attempts to leave before they finally break free? When an abuse victim attempts to flee an abusive relationship, especially with someone as emotionally volatile as the narcissist, he or she enters what may very well be the most dangerous time of his or her life. The most dangerous time in an abusive relationship is when the victim leaves. The abuser is far more likely to ramp up abuse if he feels as though his victim is slipping away from him, and he will do anything he can to get that victim back.

Further, there are several challenges that someone faces upon first leaving an abusive relationship. The victim may lack support from anyone, or the abuser may be someone prominent in the area, so no one will believe what the victim has to say. The victim may believe the threats or may stay behind or go back to protect children, particularly if the children are not physically abused. Sometimes, culture or religious norms dictate that a divorce will not be allowed. There are several reasons beyond that which may motivate a victim to go back to an abusive situation, and it is not always easy to leave, especially if the victim does not have anyone locally that can help, or does not have money or access to money.

Leaving someone you love is hard, even if there is abuse involved. It is highly likely that, at least on some level, the victim loves the narcissist, and that can be a huge motivator to return as well. The victim may convince herself that the abuse is not that bad, or believe that the narcissist will stop as he has promised. No matter the reason, it is no one's place to judge the abuse victim for going back to the narcissist if that is the choice she has made. What you should do instead is an attempt to support and encourage the victim and remind her that you are always there if she wants to talk.

If There Are No Marks, Then Are You Really Being Abused?

Abuse is not always physical, and physical abuse does not always leave a bruise. An abuser has plenty of invisible ways to abuse a victim. She could restrict funds to her victim, control communication with the outside world, threaten, manipulate, or call names. Just because there is not a physical mark does not mean that there is no harm. Oftentimes, the internal, invisible injuries that occur are far worse than anything an abuser could have inflicted physically.

Here are some of the lesser-known, invisible kinds of abuse that the victim may have endured at the hands of the narcissist:

3. Emotional abuse

4. Manipulation

5. Sexual abuse

6. Intimidation

7. Throwing items

8. Damaging the victim's items

9. Threatening

10. Financial abuse

Even physical abuse can be done in ways that do not leave marks that are visible. The narcissist could corner the victim and grab the victims face to force the victim to look at her or restrain his wrists. She could have hit him, but not hard enough to leave a mark. She could have dumped water at him, or thrown something in his general direction with the intention of hitting him but missing. Just because you do not see a mark does not mean nothing happened.

All of these actions are intended to exert control in some way, and all of them can do serious harm to one's mental wellbeing. The victim is at risk of developing anxiety, depression, or PTSD, and is at a higher risk of self-harm or suicide.

Ultimately, if someone tells you abuse is happening, the best thing you can do is acknowledge what is being said and accept it. If the victim comes to you, do not voice that you do not believe what happened. Offer whatever support you can give, even if that is none, but never discredit the victim. It already took a lot of courage for the victim to step forward and disclose to you in the first place.

But he's such a nice guy—you must have done something to really anger him if he hurt you.

No One Ever Deserves to Be Abused

This is so important; it needs to be repeated twice: No one ever deserves to be abused.

The narcissist thrives on making other people believe he is a nice guy. He wants everyone to see him as the best person ever because that is what his personality disorder dictates, he should do. He likely has delusions of grandeur, and you thinking that he is too nice to be to blame for abusing someone is exactly what he wants. Now, he does not even have to be the one to gaslight the victim—random people will do it for him!

No matter what the situation is, no one ever deserves what narcissists do. Even if the victim had cheated or even intentionally destroyed something the narcissist thought was important to him, the victim never deserves to be hit, demeaned, belittled, or abused at all.

The only person responsible for the narcissist's actions is the narcissist. The narcissist can control himself if he puts in the effort—he just chose not to. Do not defend the abuser, no matter how good of a person he may seem to be. Of course, he seems like a good guy—no intelligent abuser is going to walk around, broadcasting that he fantasizes about hurting other people. He never would have won his victim over had he started out his first date saying that he planned to smack her every time she talks back once they get about a year into the relationship.

In protecting the abuser, you are only proving that you, too, have fallen for his manipulation.

Only weak people get abused. You aren't weak.

This is yet another misconception. Anyone can find themselves in an abusive, narcissistic relationship, and most of the traits that attract narcissists are not negative, or signs of weakness. Narcissists are attracted to highly empathetic individuals, particularly those who are compassionate and patient. They want people who will want to make them feel better, and those people are often strong and independent but find themselves entirely blindsided over time.

Likewise, just because someone has been abused does not mean that he is weak. Being abused only negatively reflects upon the abuser, and not at all upon the victim.

Saying that only weak people get abused is akin to saying that only drunk people get into car accidents. While yes, some submissive people will be taken advantage of by the narcissist, they are not the only ones. Drunk people might be more likely to crash their cars by virtue of being drunk, but ultimately, far more accidents happen to sober drivers than drunk. Generalizations like this are fallacious by nature and should try to be avoided.

If he is really a narcissist, then he has a mental health issue. You can't leave him if he's mentally sick. Remember your wedding vows!

Yes, wedding vows state in sickness and in health. However, wedding values also said to love and cherish, and the narcissist did not hold up that end, either. Your wedding vows also never obligated you to stay in an abusive relationship that could do permanent harm to you.

Telling an abuse victim that they are not allowed to leave for any reason only makes it that much harder for the victim to free herself later. Remember that statistic on it taking people an average of seven attempts to leave an abuser?

That is because of people who say things like this to them, and they feel guilty for leaving. The victim is already likely grieving the relationship; there is no reason to try to guilt her into staying due to wedding vows, or due to any other reason.

Yes, the narcissist may be suffering from a personality disorder, but that is not a free pass to do whatever he wants. He cannot just decide to hurt other people because he wants to, and his personality disorder says he has a tendency to do so. That is hardly an acceptable reason to hurt someone. Likewise, the burden is on the narcissist to try to care for himself as well. If he truly wanted to get better or to learn how to live with his disorder, he would have done so. Telling the abuse victim to stay with him only enables him to continue acting the way he has been since there was no consequence.

If things are so bad, you could have left by now, couldn't you?

Yes, in theory, but not necessarily in reality.

Leaving a relationship, particularly a marriage involving a house and children involves a lot of bureaucracy, which, in turn, requires a lot of money. If the victim lacks access to money, or the victim has children, leaving is never as simple as just walking out the door and never seeing the narcissist again. Return to the first stereotype to see a long list of reasons why a person may choose to stay in an abusive relationship.

What about the children? They need both parents in their lives.

Children need healthy parents in their lives. Growing up in an environment with two parents fighting constantly is worse for the child than growing up in two separate houses. Even with a narcissistic parent, with one emotionally healthy parent there to help guide the children through the fog of dealing with a narcissist, many children will do just fine. They are better off seeing their parents separate and not fighting, and their own mental health will thank them for it. Think of it this way—if you stay married to an abusive narcissist, your children will come to internalize that as what to expect in their own marriages, oftentimes taking the role of whichever parent is the same gender as them. If you do not want your children to grow up to be abusers or abuse victims, you are doing them a huge favor by getting out of the relationship.

Domestic violence is a private matter between partners and should be left behind closed doors.

No.

If you ever hear domestic violence or suspect that you hear domestic violence, the right thing to do is always to call emergency services. Domestic violence claims the lives of at least 30,000 people a year. Your call to emergency services could save a life. Even if you are unsure, even just reporting it means that someone else can investigate and make sure everyone is safe.

If you are worried about retaliation, you can make sure to emphasize that you want to remain anonymous to the people on whom you are calling. Oftentimes, there are ways to allow for that, and the police will likely be sympathetic to you not wanting to start a feud with a neighbor, especially if that neighbor is already getting phone calls for domestic violence.

Just because you are not actively witnessing the abuse and just because it is occurring behind closed doors does not mean you should ignore it. Protect your neighbors. Save a life. Always call in if you suspect domestic violence.

Acknowledging Abuse

You may have heard that you can't find love until you learn to love yourself. This is often true of most things. You can't learn to be patient with others until you learn to be patient with yourself. Sure, you might be more patient with others than you are yourself already. Yet, you'll find that when you fail at being patient with others, it is most likely a failure because you have absolutely no patience with yourself when it comes to that particular kind of mistake.

I have a family member who is always early to everything. That same family member has absolutely no patience for tardiness. I am sure you have examples like this as well. The point is that we often have less patience for others when it comes to matters of which we are not patient with ourselves. One way to find patience with yourself is to ask yourself about your own intentions.

Often times, we request forgiveness because our intention was not aimed toward harm. You might say you're sorry but you did not mean to offend. What you mean is that it was not your intention to cause offense. In this case, you apologize and request forgiveness for that apology based upon the explanation that you did not mean to offend.

When you make a mistake, ask yourself if you meant to make that mistake. If you did, you might have some further reckoning to do with yourself. If you didn't, you might approach yourself the way you would approach someone else who made an unintentional mistake. Or, you could approach yourself the way you would want someone else to approach your unintentional mistake—with forgiveness.

It's a strange thought, I realize. Being patient with others requires learning to be patient with yourself, and being patient with yourself requires treating yourself with the kind of patience you treat others. It seems paradoxical, I know. What it actually accomplishes, however, is the resolution of a paradox.

A paradox is something that seems contradictory but somehow is not. It seems contradictory that you'd need to learn to be patient with yourself to be patient with others because you're naturally more patient with others. It isn't actually a contradiction, though.

It means that if you take your more natural disposition to be patient and apply it to yourself, you'll be even more patient with others because you'll resolve those instances of complete inability to be patient with yourself. You'll resolve your failures in times of patience.

Again, your failures when it comes to patience can usually be linked to those instances in which you afford yourself no patience. If you can afford yourself no patience for tardiness, you will be unable to afford others patience either. This isn't necessarily a bad thing. You could live a completely fulfilled life without patience for tardiness. The point is not about the matter.

The point is that the more patience you show yourself, the more patience you'll show others. Since you naturally show more patience to others than yourself, show yourself the kind of patience you show others. Once you've allowed yourself more patience, you will find you have more patience for others. It's that simple (or, that complicated). In either case, you can do it.

There are a multitude of activities you can do to improve upon your patience with yourself. Your patience with yourself is crucial for your ability to recover and develop new relationships.

It is important that you learn to guard yourself from entering into another relationship with a narcissist but it is also important that you do not become so impatient with anything that reminds you of the narcissist in your last relationship that you struggle to form new relationships.

The world is a more stimulating place than the narcissist you were with made it feel. You will need to come up with new activities to find yourself in the world again. The relationship you were in with a narcissist attacked your sense of identity, boundaries, reality, and control. You will need to actively participate in activities that put you back to a place where you can reclaim your sense of identity and control.

Your goal is to find activities to reestablish what was taken from you. You will want to reestablish your boundaries. You will want to reclaim your identity. You will want to find a relationship in which reciprocation is readily available and understood as important.

You have the tools in your home, neighborhood, and backyard to reestablish your boundaries. Actively pursue the reinstatement of your boundaries. You have the tools to reclaim your identity. Actively pursue your own sense of self. Recognize how it was stifled and how you can get it back.

Admitting that there has been a problem in your life that caused you to lose your sense of identity will be crucial for your recovery. You must get out into the world and find your place again. You must reclaim it without the narcissist you were in a relationship with previously.

Yoga is a great way to stimulate a fruitful connection between mind, body, and one's surroundings in people who might not be ready to become active in institutionalized sports and other such strenuous activities. This is the perfect example of a theme you could take so far beyond the ten poses offered in this book.

The ten poses offered were selected because they promote mindfulness which will help you reclaim your identity as you work toward mindfulness of yourself and your body's needs. The narcissist you were in a relationship with disrespected your body's boundaries and your mind's need for human connection and grounding in reality. It is time for you to find activities that tie you to the ground again and help you look inward.

Like yoga or anything else, mindfulness can be practiced and honed; it just takes a conscious effort. Conscientiousness is mindfulness, after all. You will hone mindfulness as soon as you start doing activities for yourself again. You simply have to do the work to articulate the experience and provide yourself with the understanding that you are doing things for yourself again.

These activities are meant to give you ideas to instigate theses experience and to inspire a reclamation of identity. Use them well but feel free to create your own experiences along the way. The point is simply to get started conscientiously.

You'll find that mindfulness/conscientiousness inspires self-reflection. If you have wondered how anyone can teach self-reflection, you've asked a great question. Some people seem to be turned inward. Others seem to be turned outward. We all seem to have the potential to change our gaze, though.

When you were with a narcissist, both of you gazed into them. Now it is time for you to start practicing gazing inward toward yourself and then outward toward other things than the narcissist that convinced you that your gaze was most worthwhile when it was on them.

Self-awareness is an important part of life. Children become self-conscious at a scary point in their life. We use the word self-conscious colloquially to mean something like bashful or socially anxious. Its literal meaning is essentially to be self-aware—to be aware of one's self as a self. Any child will become self-aware and self-conscious (both meanings now apply) without much warning. It is important that, when this happens, they know how to self-reflect and then speak to others about their self-reflections.

This is how we move between turning inward and turning outward. What you will be learning to do once again is honor your self-awareness and your ability to turn inward and outward. The reason for this is that you have had your gaze turned toward the narcissist for a long time. It is time to turn it toward yourself and others.

Some people get stuck in their inward lives. Struggles that result from this are numerous. This can make relationships challenging. It can make holding a job challenging. It is crucial to your recovery that you neither get stuck retreating totally back into yourself nor outward without reclaiming your sense of identity. The narcissist you were with was empty inside. He or she tried to empty you out too. Don't be like them. You have to find the substance within yourself without forgetting to do what the narcissist struggled to do—look outside of yourself too. You need to make these passages. You need to find yourself without getting stuck there.

Technology is precisely mediation, which makes it the opposite of immediacy. Technology is a go-between. Someone creates something for us.

We do not have to engage in the world directly. We get to do it directly. We may not be able to speak with someone directly but with a social media app we can speak with them indirectly.

We can even spy on someone, making the experience overtly indirect. They don't have to know we are looking into their lives and interests because we can peek into their lives and interests indirectly.

The truth is that narcissists are good at hiding what they are ashamed of. They cannot handle shame so they do not want to feel it. They will avoid it. If they were ashamed of their parent who was a narcissist, they might be especially good at hiding. You must think of the surprise outbursts and the abuse you did experience. Otherwise, you won't ever feel like you're reading the right book.

If you are sure by now that you were in a relationship with a narcissist, regardless of their ability to hide it from you occasionally, it is time for you to move towards acceptance of your abuse. Only once you accept the abuse you experienced can you move past it. It is time for you to acknowledge it and face reality in the way the narcissist could not.

You must undo the issues they caused due to the issues they had. First, you should realize that they may have passed on some of their tendencies to you. In other words, you might also now experience a difficulty to deal with shame, accept reality, put up boundaries, and have reciprocal relationships. You will need to get over these issues in order to recover.

Your Reaction to Shame After Narcissistic Abuse

Depending upon how long you were with a narcissist, you may have picked up on their defense mechanisms when it comes to shame. You might now be experiencing a kind of shame you are no better equipped to deal with than the narcissist was. You might be ashamed of yourself to falling victim to a narcissist. This is understandable.

If you have been reading this book and thinking on the one hand that you were definitely in a relationship with a narcissist and that, on the other hand, it was never so obvious then as it is now, it is important that you learn to accept that you are not special.

Your relationship with a narcissist was no more special than the narcissist was. A narcissist thinks they're special. If you think your relationship with this particular narcissist was special, you have fallen victim to thinking like the narcissist you were with.

Acknowledge the reality of your relationship. It was great at first. Narcissists are attractive for many reasons. Forgive yourself for being attracted. It's an attractive thing. Narcissists appear seductively aloof. Their lack of boundaries appears intimate.

Their unquenchable thirst for affirmation makes them appear as though they simply need your love to be whole. If you're an empath, you had every reason to want to help the narcissist you were in a relationship. It is important that you realize that you were duped but that doesn't mean you have to hate yourself.

Admit it. You aren't special. Your relationship with a narcissist was not special. No one is that special. If you were really special, you would be hearing all of this from someone more important than the author of this book. The point of accepting this is avoiding the sins of narcissism yourself.

The narcissist you were with could have been really good at tricking you but that does not mean that you were not tricked. Admit that you are "trickable." Admit that you are fallible. Admit that you are human. Accept this and get ready to move on. Don't be a narcissist. Don't deny your reality.

If this abuse fits your experience, accept that and learn to move on. If you keep criticizing books because they don't describe a narcissist as talented as yours, you aren't helping yourself. You're falling victim to narcissistic thinking. Accept the reality of your situation so that you can move on in a way that they can't.

The Need for Psychological Help

A personality of a person is shaped by experiences, environment, and inherited characteristics. But once the person behaves in an unusual way such as becoming aggressive, egoistic, and insensitive, then that person possibly has a personality disorder. For someone who is diagnosed with this illness, a lot of factors are considered to be the reasons contributing to such. This can also cause distress over a long period. In the 21st century, the most prevalent disorder case is Narcissistic Personality Disorder (NDP). This is one of the many mental illnesses that can destroy one's life if not being controlled. Someone with NDP tends to project an attention-seeker attitude. This is common to the younger generation or what we mostly refer to as

Millennials.

Narcissistic people regard themselves as someone with dominating power. They usually disregard others. When they feel the urge to demean or insult people, they will not hesitate. They can even pose as the kind of people you never wish to interact with. They are manipulative in some ways, and often just showoff themselves to the many. If you know someone with this attitude, it is really frustrating to act nicely around them.

However, even though they are annoying, we still do not know what made them act like that. According to some psychologists, people with Narcissistic Personality Disorder may have lived a miserable life, especially as a child. They have probably experienced neglection in the past. They might have never gotten the things they wanted during their childhood days. As they grow older, the feelings of wanting to be appreciated, admired, and accepted may have pushed them to put a mask to hide their pain. As you see, people with personality illnesses are the loneliest. They are the people who may suffer from anxiety and depression. They act tough, but they can be the most vulnerable people hiding in shadows.

If you know someone with a narcissistic personality disorder, or you think you are in the same boat with them, it is necessary to try seeking help from the experts in the psychological field. Some people might think that there is no need for psychological intervention, but they are mistaken. Talking to experts about your countless problems and your situation will grant you the enlightenment to get better. They can help you overcome the factors affecting the personality that inhibits you from achieving psychological health.

People with Narcissistic Personality Disorder requires immediate and thorough psychological aid because this can lead to suicide, depression, physical abuse, and drug abuse. However, confirmed NPD patients do not actively seek help themselves. This is for the reason that they strongly believe that nothing is wrong with them. Not until their disorder starts to impact their lives significantly. Even though these people are on the verge of major depression and suicide, they still would not consider asking for medical help. They pride themselves in being perfect. They believe that it would be detrimental to their public image when they start going to psychological therapy. They Are afraid that others will look down to them, thinking that they have gone crazy. So, they prefer to hide everything to themselves than speaking up to a psychological expert or therapist.   They do not want to look like a loser in front of their friends and family. People with NPD strives to continue to fit in as well to be accepted by society. They will put on a gallant mask so no one will know their weakness.

There are actual cases of NDP that involves the abuse of drugs to satisfy their neurotic needs and escape from the reality that people keep on reiterating to them. Others even try to end their suffering by physically abusing themselves, which could be in the form of starvation, cutting of wrists, and even suicide.

The real question is, "Why do people tend to fear psychological help?" The answer lies in one simple word – stigma. Even if people say, "There is no stigma about psychological help anymore," some people will remain with their false beliefs. Sadly, despite the countless movements and seminars to raise mental awareness all over the world, there will always be those who think that seeking psychological help is a form of weakness and psychoticism. This is the only psychological disorder they are aware of. The rest forms of abnormal behavior seem to be just a part of an attitude that can be fixed through punishment and confrontation. What they cannot fathom is that there is a medical basis for how people acquire psychological disorders such as depression, anxiety disorder, and phobia. MRI scans show an abnormality on the brain structure when a person has a disorder. Saying that, "Depression is only on your mind" is like saying to a cancer patient that, "Cancer is just a phantom illness." There is a physiological reason behind these psychological abnormalities. To some people, this is just attitude. But medically speaking, psychological disorders are the brain versions of cancer, and the end game is death either from suicide, aggression, or impulsivity.

If you are suffering from any of the psychological disorders, or if you know someone who is suffering the same fate, never hesitate to contact a competent psychologist or a psychotherapist. Help the movement to raise awareness that psychological intervention is not only for psychosis. It is to help people solve even the most basic problems in society such as bullying, marriage problems, family problems, even identity crisis. Psychological intervention is not only focused on grave psychological conditions. Rather, it is for all people who aim to acquire a healthy psychological state and personality. Here are some tips on how you can ward off the stigma of ignorant people towards psychological interventions:

1. Be Open about Mental Health. When people dissuade you from going to a psychologist because they believe that you will be paying a lot of money for nothing, open to them that mental health is important to you and none of your methods to acquire it is working. You will need a psychologist or a psychotherapist to help you regain psychological health. Educate them properly about what happens during a psychological intervention. The psychologist is there to help you open your problems up so you can understand what you're feeling and what you're thinking. He or she can help you sort these unwanted forces that are driving you to confusion and distortion. With the help of several therapies, make them understand that they are the only people who can uncover your unconscious to uncover the negative roots of your personality and foster a more positive mindset towards healing and growth.

2. Educate them about the equality between physical illness and mental illness. Tell them that the body and mind are interconnected, and they affect one another. By curing your psychological disorder, it might help you heal from your physiological illnesses such as hypertension, weakened immune system, diabetes, and others.

3. If you are ashamed about what people are saying behind your back, choose empowerment. Take this as your motivation to your big and healthy comeback. The next time they see you, you will be ten times more psychologically healthy than they are. Finally, you can foster healing, and you can develop holistically as a person.

You do not have to deprive yourself of psychological help just because you are afraid to be judged and called crazy by the people around you. Don't you want to feel happiness, competence, satisfaction, and confidence within yourself? Don't you want to be able to build intimate and long-lasting relationships? Honestly, it is you who are making it hard for yourself if you keep denying this need. Without treatment, you will remain unproductive and inefficient. The worst part is, your condition might worsen and might get you to develop more disorders in the future.

Even if you can continue to live with NDP or any other psychological disorder, take note that your abilities and potentials will be limited as you deal with the complications of this disorder. It will affect you not only physically and mentally but also socially, as you push others away through disparaging manners. Soon enough, you are going to feel loneliness, despair, and you will remain secluded from the rest of the world.

Narcissism can only be defused by stepping back and stepping on your ego. You have the power to change who you are to a positive light. Ask yourself who you want to be and what you like to do. Stick to it like it is your dream. The first step to reach it is to acquire a psychologically healthy personality. With the help of mental health professionals, you can unleash your capabilities as an individual, and soon enough, you will have the undying power to reach your timely success and happiness.

It will not be easy in the beginning. But with passion, time, courage, and determination, you can get out of the prison of your own mind. There is always a way back to your real self. Start by asking for medical help. Once you can overcome your narcissistic personality, you will finally be able to get the genuine love and happiness you want. It may take time and constant effort, but never give up no matter how tiring it gets. After all, the best person that can help you get out of your unhealthy situation is yourself. You exist with a purpose, with the help of psychological intervention, everything will fall into place. All you need is to have faith in yourself and on the process.

Key Points: There will always be a need for psychological evaluation and intervention. People will not be innovated such process if there is no need for it. Psychological help is not only for people with disorders or psychosis. It is time to break the stigma in your society that psychological help is for all people who want to get over their self-defeating tendencies and have a more definite goal in life.

Call to Action: Do not be ashamed when people only you out of seeking psychological help. It is not them you are trying to fix, but your own thinking. Instead of ruminating on those negative feelings, voice them out to people nicely. Make them understand that psychological help will heal you from your mental and psychological malfunctions. So, when you get out of there, it will be like a brand new you - better, more likable, and bolder to achieve your dreams someday.

CHAPTER 15

BUILDING DAILY POSITIVE BEHAVIORS

USING MEDITATION, MANTRAS, AND POSITIVE AFFIRMATIONS

As you continue on your journey toward healing and freeing yourself from the narcissist, you may feel times where you need some extra self-care or quiet to really focus on yourself and reflect on everything. When this happens, and you feel the need to seek out quiet, you should try using one of these methods. Meditations, mantras, and positive affirmations can all be quite beneficial as you attempt to heal from the narcissist, and they can help you in moments of weakness or self-doubt when you are not sure if you are doing the right thing. Through these methods, you will be able to return yourself to a quiet state of calmness that can aid you in returning to a state of relaxation and clear-headedness.

Meditation

Meditation happens when you focus on positivity. You seek to center yourself in a feeling of positivity in order to drown out the negative feelings. If you are feeling upset about the abuse you have endured, for example, and are feeling unworthy due to the abuse, worried that you will never find someone who wants to be with you because you feel that you are too broken to ever be a viable partner, you may feel like your mind is running a million miles a minute. It is, in a sense—your negative thoughts and feelings are spiraling out of control, and you are struggling to reel them in.

When you meditate, you instead attempt to quiet your mind by focusing on something positive. Rather than focusing on feeling unlovable, you may focus on the feeling of being in love and of loving yourself. You let yourself shift from that negative place to one rooted in positivity, in which you feel yourself relaxing. Over time, you may begin to feel as though you are lovable, and you recognize that you love yourself, which means you must be lovable. Ultimately, the goal when you attempt to meditate is to shift your mind from the negative thought cycles and patterns to positive ones. The more you practice, the easier it becomes to shift to that quiet place in your mind where you feel calm and safe, even in the face of danger or your greatest fears.

How to meditate

When you are ready to meditate, you must first prepare. You cannot just rush straight into attempting to reach a meditative state. Instead, you must start by locating a quiet place. You need somewhere calm and quiet, so you will not find yourself being pulled out of the meditative state you are trying to reach every time something happens around you.

After locating your meditation space, you should get into a comfortable position. Sit down, cross-legged, and straighten your back out. Your back should be straightened into the proper posture for your spine, but you should not feel tense. As you sit there, take a few deep breaths as you encourage yourself to relax.

As you begin to relax, focus on a positive wish of some sort. It can benefit yourself or other people. It could be a wish for healing as you focus your thoughts; you may focus on how you hope that your mind and body will begin to heal from the narcissist's abuse. Keep this wish, this hope for healing, in mind as you continue to meditate. Focus on healing, positive energy as you stay in your relaxed state, and attempt to memorize that feeling.

As you come out of your meditative state, dedicate the positive feelings you have created, and that positive energy generated, to yourself and those you love, wishing them the best. As you go about your day, remember those feelings to ground yourself when you feel stress coming or to use to guide yourself through your day, making sure the actions you choose are related to the feelings you generated during meditation.

Mantras

Mantras are quite related to meditation—they are words that you use to keep yourself concentrated on your meditations. They allow you to regroup and focus back on your meditations if you were to get distracted. When you are trying to heal from narcissistic abuse, you can use these mantras to redirect your mind when you are beginning to feel distracted or overwhelmed. When feelings of negativity, worthlessness, or just hurt are threatening to overwhelm you, it is difficult to get out of that rut. You may feel as though you have no way to get out of the situation, and when that happens, you can repeat a phrase, or a mantra, to yourself to regroup.

Creating mantras

Creating a mantra is an immensely personal task. It can be quite difficult to do if you do not know what you are doing or you are unsure how to create something truly meaningful to you and your situation. When you are ready to create your mantra, take a journal or a sheet of paper and a pen and find a quiet location where you can focus for the next thirty minutes without distractions. This is the most effective when you do it in the morning when your mind is not yet overwhelmed with the dozens of worries you may feel throughout your day. First, begin by identifying something that you will need a mantra for. For the narcissistic abuse survivor, this may be something about healing, self-worth, or self-esteem. You should then focus on that one thing that you want to attain. If you wish to attain healing, you may think about those healing feelings you felt when meditation and how you want to be able to return to that state of calmness. Write in your journal about everything and anything that comes to mind regarding healing from the abuse. Take thirty minutes to free-write without distraction.

When your writing time is over, take a few moments to go over everything you have written and attempt to condense it down into one sentence or word. If you wrote about how you want your mind to heal from the narcissist's abuse, you could write something along the lines of, "I am ready to let go of the pain and welcome happiness and loving energy into my life."

You can then use this in moments of stress when those feelings from the abuse threaten to overwhelm you, and also attempt to integrate them into your meditations. The more you use them in conjunction with your meditations, the more you may begin to feel as though they are becoming associated with the feelings of calmness and healing you were feeling during your meditation.

Examples

Take things at your own pace: When you have lived a life of being abused by the narcissist when you do not tend to his needs immediately after he has asked for you to do so, you may attempt to move quicker than necessary. You are trying to compensate for the fact that he may want multiple things at once that also clash with you meeting your own needs. Because of this, you may have gotten into the habit of rushing yourself. A mantra such as this one reminds you that it is okay to slow down sometimes. It reminds you to be mindful of what is happening around you and to take things at a natural pace rather than forcing things to go quicker than necessary.

I am not ashamed of myself: Oftentimes, narcissistic abuse victims find themselves hiding. They, like the narcissist, do not want the outside world to see who they are because they fear the judgment they may face. You may try to hide your pain behind a brave face, hiding your abuse and attempting to minimize the effects the narcissist may have had on you. However, this defeats the entire purpose of healing—you are allowed to be you, even if the you that you are right now is injured and in need of healing. Do not be ashamed to show your scars. They are the marks that you have survived, and you should be proud of them, not ashamed.

Positive Affirmations

Affirmations are sentences you speak to yourself to remind you to take a certain mindset or action for positive daily behaviors. Like the mantra, they are short and personalized, but rather than encompassing a goal or desired result; the affirmations are triggers to act or think in a certain way that is conducive to positivity. When spoken to yourself, preferably out loud, so you hear the words, these affirmations aid in shifting how you are thinking at that moment and empower you.

These affirmations are like support for the foundations of your mind—they keep you strong in moments of weakness, and over time, the more you repeat them to yourself, the truer they become to you at the moment. Over time, you will find yourself less vulnerable toward the negativity that you had tried to protect yourself against in the first place, and you will find yourself needing to rely on the affirmations less and less during your journey toward healing.

Creating affirmations

When you are trying to create your affirmations, they must follow a certain structure. They must be:

- Positive: All affirmations must be worded in a positive

manner to really reinforce the idea that you will be shifting your thinking into positivity.

- Present tense: Your affirmation must be in the present tense to make it more difficult to deny or reject. By wording things positively, you are saying that they are true at that particular moment.

- Brief and specific: Your affirmation should be something short, but specific to whatever it is that you are attempting to correct within yourself. Short means it is easier for you to remember at the moment while specific means you should be able to use it for its intended purpose.

- Active: Your affirmation should include a word that ends in "-ing" to show that it is an active affirmation. This reminds you that you are actively doing something, and will cue you to do so.

- About you: You are the only thing in this world that you have control over. As such, you should make sure your affirmation focuses on you when you make it. You will be able to say that it is true because you can make it so.

Examples of affirmations

I am healing, even if it is a slow process: This reminds you that you are working toward achieving health and wellness. You are actively working to better yourself and heal, and even when you feel as though you are not, or that you have taken a step backward, or failed in some way, this affirmation will remind you that you are a work-in-progress, and that is okay. It is okay for the healing process to be slow. It is okay for you to have setbacks sometimes.

I am trustworthy, and I am willing to rely on my perceptions of reality: Remember how the narcissist loves to gaslight victims? It can be incredibly useful to remind yourself that you are trustworthy, even if the narcissist has attempted to convince you otherwise. Whenever you are beginning to doubt whether you understand what is happening, you can repeat this affirmation to yourself.

I am able to support my boundaries, and I am protecting them any time

they are challenged: This reminds you to protect your own boundaries. Remember, boundaries are created to make some sort of distance between yourself and another person in an effort to protect yourself. If you are protecting your own boundaries, you are essentially insisting that they are honored and your limits are protected. This can be difficult after having lived with a narcissist that would frequently push back at your boundaries and refuse to respect them.

I am prioritizing my own self-care: This reminds you that sometimes, you need to put yourself first. Sometimes, it is appropriate and important to tell other people no and tend to yourself. Your self-care keeps your mind and body happy and healthy and therefore, tended to. Ultimately, you are responsible for yourself, and you need to take that responsibility seriously because no one else will do it for you. Even if the narcissist has taught you to fear caring for yourself, it must be done for your own sake and for the sake of any who may rely on you for care, such as children or pets.

CONCLUSION

Congratulations on reading Narcissistic Abuse book. You are well on your way to answering all of the questions that you have had about your own partnership or other experiences so that you can survive the narcissistic relationship and recover and heal from it.

This book has been a guide to show you all you need to know to feel empowered to take control of your life by being able to understand and identify what a narcissist is and how they operate, where narcissism comes from and some of the hallmark traits and characteristics of the narcissist.

You have also been shown what a codependent partnership can look like, why empaths and narcissists are drawn to each other romantically, and an overall sense of what the narcissistic relationship pattern looks like. Creating awareness in all these matters is what will help you learn how to survive the experience and follow through with healing the issues of such a partnership.

This book has given you understanding, information about what narcissistic abuse looks like, and what it can do to a person as well as how it can influence the whole family, especially young and developing children.

With all of this comes the honesty that you may need to prove your courage and find your way forward, as this book helps you see that there are easy ways to find help and support to guide you forward in your recovery. Once you have been able to identify the issues and causes of some of your relationship and personal problems, you can then provide the right movement forward for your healing and recovery.

This guide wants to support you all the way through, no matter what decisions you decide to make with your partnership and yourself. You are brave, strong, and courageous for taking this first big step in reading about the narcissistic relationship and as you move forward, use this book as a form of help and support to keep you informed, motivated and balanced as you work through surviving the narcissistic relationship. Good luck on the road ahead, and remember, you are not alone.

www.ingramcontent.com/pod-product-compliance
Lightning Source LLC
Chambersburg PA
CBHW062233150726
47991CB00006B/2555